ORACLE DATABASE 12C ADMINISTRATION EXAM PRACTICE QUESTIONS & DUMPS

220+ Practice Tests for Oracle 1Z0-062
Updated 2020

Presented By: Emerald Books

About Emerald Books:

Emerald Books is a publishing house based in Hudson, Texas, USA, a platform that is available both online & locally, which unleashes the power of educational content, literary collection, poetry & many other book genres. We make it easy for writers & authors to get their books designed, published, promoted, and sell professionally on worldwide scale with eBook + Print distribution. Emerald Books was founded in 2015, and is now distributing books worldwide.

QUESTION 1

Examine the parameters for your database instance:

NAME	TYPE	VALUE
undo_management	string	AUTO
undo_retention	integer	1200
undo_tablespace	string	UNDOTBS1

You execute the following command:

```
SQL> ALTER TABLESPACE undotbs1 RETENTION NOGUARANTEE;
```

Which statement is true in this scenario?

A. Undo data is written to flashback logs after 1200 seconds.
B. Inactive undo data is retained for 1200 seconds even if subsequent transactions fail due to lack of space in the undo tablespace.
C. You can perform a Flashback Database operation only within the duration of 1200 seconds.
D. An attempt is made to keep inactive undo for 1200 seconds but transactions may overwrite the undo before that time has elapsed.

Correct Answer: D

QUESTION 2

As a user of the ORCL database, you establish a database link to the remote HQ database such that all users in the ORCL database may access tables only from the SCOTT schema in the HQ database. SCOTT's password is TIGER. The service mane "HQ" is used to connect to the remote HQ database.

Which command would you execute to create the database link?

A. CREATE DATABASE LINK HQ USING 'HQ';
B. CREATE DATABASE LINK HQ CONNECT TO CURRENT_USER USING 'HQ';

C. CREATE PUBLIC DATABASE LINK HQ CONNECT TO scott
    IDENTIFIED BY tiger USING 'HQ';
D. CREATE DATABASE LINK HQ CONNECT TO scott IDENTIFIED BY
    tiger USING 'HQ';

Correct Answer: C

QUESTION 3

You plan to create a database by using the Database Configuration
Assistant (DBCA), with the following specifications:

– Applications will connect to the database via a middle tier.
– The number of concurrent user connections will be high.
– The database will have mixed workload, with the execution of complex BI
queries scheduled at night. Which DBCA option must you choose to create
the database?

A. a General Purpose database template with default memory allocation
B. a Data Warehouse database template, with the dedicated server mode
    option and AMM enabled
C. a General Purpose database template, with the shared server mode
    option and Automatic MemoryManagement (AMM) enabled
D. a default database configuration

Correct Answer: C

QUESTION 4

Which two statements correctly describe the relationship between data files
and logical database structures? (Choose two.)

A. A segment cannot span data files.
B. A data file can belong to only one tablespace.
C. An extent cannot span data files.
D. The size of an Oracle data block in a data file should be the same as
    the size of an OS block.

Correct Answer: BC

Explanation:

A single extent can never span data files.
https://docs.oracle.com/database/121/CNCPT/logical.htm#CNCPT1095

QUESTION 5

Which two tasks can be performed on an external table? (Choose two.)

A. partitioning the table
B. creating an invisible index
C. updating the table by using an update statement
D. creating a public synonym
E. creating a view

Correct Answer: DE

Explanation/Reference:
:
http://docs.oracle.com/cd/B28359_01/server.111/b28310/tables013.htm#AD
MIN01507

You can, for example select, join, or sort external table data. You can also create views and synonyms for external tables. However, no DML operations (UPDATE, INSERT, or DELETE) are possible, and no indexes can be created, on external tables.

QUESTION 6

Which three statements are true about a job chain? (Choose three.)

A. It can contain a nested chain of jobs.
B. It can be used to implement dependency-based scheduling.
C. It cannot invoke the same program or nested chain in multiple steps in the chain.
D. It cannot have more than one dependency.
E. It can be executed using event-based or time-based schedules.

Correct Answer: ABE

QUESTION 7

Which three factors influence the optimizer's choice of an execution plan?
(Choose three.)

A. the optimizer_mode initialization parameter
B. operating system (OS) statistics
C. cardinality estimates
D. object statistics in the data dictionary
E. fixed baselines

Correct Answer: ACD

QUESTION 8

Examine the resources consumed by a database instance whose current
Resource Manager plan is displayed.

```
SQL> SELECT name, active_sessions, queue_length,
        consumed_cpu_time, cpu_waits, cpu_wait_time
     FROM v$rsrc_consumer_group;

NAME            ACTIVE_SESSIONS   QUEUE_LENGTH   CONSUMED_CPU_WAITS   CPU_WAITS
CPU_WAIT_TIME
-----------     -------------     -----------    ----------------     -------  -----
----

OLTP__ORDER__ENTRY      1               0                  29690           467
6709
OTHES__GROUPS           0               0                5982366          4089
60425
SYS_GROUP               1               0                2420704           914
19540
DSS_QUERIES             4               2                4594660          3004
55700
```

Which two statements are true? (Choose two.)

A. An attempt to start a new session by a user belonging to
   DSS_QUERIES fails with an error.
B. An attempt to start a new session by a user belonging to
   OTHER_GROUPS fails with an error.
C. The CPU_WAIT_TIME column indicates the total time that sessions in
   the consumer group waited for the CPU due to resource management.
D. The CPU_WAIT_TIME column indicates the total time that sessions in

the consumer group waited for the CPU due to I/O waits and latch or enqueue contention.
E. A user belonging to the DSS QUERIES resource consumer group can create a new session but the session will be queued.

Correct Answer: CE

QUESTION 9

Which action takes place when a file checkpoint occurs?

A. The checkpoint position is advanced in the checkpoint queue.
B. All buffers for a checkpointed file that were modified before a specific SCN are written to disk by DBWn and the SCN is stored in the control file.
C. The Database Writer process (DBWn) writes all dirty buffers in the buffer cache to data files.
D. The Log Writer process (LGWR) writes all redo entries in the log buffer to online redo log files.

Correct Answer: B

QUESTION 10

Examine the structure of the sales table, which is stored in a locally managed tablespace with Automatic Segment Space Management (ASSM) enabled.

Name	Null?	Type
PROD_ID	NOT NULL	NUMBER
CUST_ID	NOT NULL	NUMBER
TIME_ID	NOT NULL	DATE
CHANNEL_ID	NOT NULL	NUMBER
PROMO_ID	NOT NULL	NUMBER
QUANTITY_SOLD	NOT NULL	NUMBER (10,2)
AMOUNT_SOLD	NOT NULL	NUMBER (10,2)

You want to perform online segment shrink to reclaim fragmented free space below the high water mark. What should you ensure before the start of the operation?

A. Row movement is enabled.
B. Referential integrity constraints for the table are disabled.
C. No queries are running on this table.
D. Extra disk space equivalent to the size of the segment is available in the tablespace.
E. No pending transaction exists on the table.

Correct Answer: A

QUESTION 11

Which statement is true regarding the startup of a database instance?

A. The instance does not start up normally and requires manual media recovery after a shutdown using the abort option.
B. Uncommitted transactions are rolled back during the startup of the database instance after a shutdown using the immediate option.
C. There is no difference in the underlying mechanics of the startup whether the database is shut down by using the immediate option or the abort option.
D. Media recovery is required when the database is shut down by using either the immediate option or the abort option.
E. Instance recovery is not required if the database instance was shut down by using SHUTDOWN IMMEDIATE.

Correct Answer: E

Explanation/Reference:

http://docs.oracle.com/cd/A87860_01/doc/server.817/a76956/start.htm

QUESTION 12

Examine the memory-related parameters set in the SPFILE of an Oracle database:

```
memory_max_target=6G
memory_target=5G
pga_aggregate_target=500M
sga_max_size=0
sga_target=0
```

Which statement is true?

A. Only SGA components are sized automatically.
B. Memory is dynamically re-allocated between the SGA and PGA as needed.
C. The size of the PGA cannot grow automatically beyond 500 MB.
D. The value of the MEMORY_TARGET parameter cannot be changed dynamically.

Correct Answer: B

QUESTION 13

Which two statements are true about extents? (Choose two.)

A. Blocks belonging to an extent can be spread across multiple data files.
B. Data blocks in an extent are logically contiguous but can be non-contiguous on disk.
C. The blocks of a newly allocated extent, although free, may have been used before.
D. Data blocks in an extent are automatically reclaimed for use by other objects in a tablespace when all the rows in a table are deleted.

Correct Answer:

QUESTION 14

You execute the commands:

```
SQL>CREATE USER sidney
    IDENTIFIED BY out_standing1
    DEFAULT TABLESPACE users
    QUOTA 10M ON users
    TEMPORARY TABLESPACE temp
    ACCOUNT UNLOCK;

SQL> GRANT CREATE SESSION TO sidney;
```

Which two statements are true? (Choose two.)

A. The `create user` command fails if any role with the name Sidney exists in the database.
B. The user `Sidney` can connect to the database instance but cannot perform sort operations because no space quota is specified for the `temp` tablespace.
C. The user `Sidney` is created but cannot connect to the database instance because no profile is default.
D. The user `Sidney` can connect to the database instance but requires relevant privileges to create objects in the `users` tablespace.
E. The user `Sidney` is created and authenticated by the operating system.

Correct Answer: AD

QUESTION 15

Your database supports a DSS workload that involves the execution of complex queries: Currently, the library cache contains the ideal workload for analysis. You want to analyze some of the queries for an application that are cached in the library cache.

What must you do to receive recommendations about the efficient use of indexes and materialized views to improve query performance?

A. Create a SQL Tuning Set (STS) that contains the queries cached in the library cache and run the SQL Tuning Advisor (STA) on the workload captured in the STS.
B. Run the Automatic Workload Repository Monitor (ADDM).
C. Create an STS that contains the queries cached in the library cache and run the SQL Performance Analyzer (SPA) on the workload captured in the STS.
D. Create an STS that contains the queries cached in the library cache and run the SQL Access Advisor on the workload captured in the STS.

Correct Answer: D

Explanation/Reference:

* SQL Access Advisor is primarily responsible for making schema modification recommendations, such as adding or dropping indexes and

materialized views. SQL Tuning Advisor makes other types of recommendations, such as creating SQL profiles and restructuring SQL statements.

* The query optimizer can also help you tune SQL statements. By using SQL Tuning Advisor and SQL Access Advisor, you can invoke the query optimizer in advisory mode to examine a SQL statement or set of statements and determine how to improve their efficiency. SQL Tuning Advisor and SQL Access Advisor can make various recommendations, such as creating SQL profiles, restructuring SQL statements, creating additional indexes or materialized views, and refreshing optimizer statistics.

Note:
* Decision support system (DSS) workload
* The library cache is a shared pool memory structure that stores executable SQL and PL/SQL code. This cache contains the shared SQL and PL/SQL areas and control structures such as locks and library cache handles.

QUESTION 16

Examine this command:

SQL > exec DBMS_STATS.SET_TABLE_PREFS ('SH', 'CUSTOMERS', 'PUBLISH', 'false');

Which three statements are true about the effect of this command? (Choose three.)

A. Statistics collection is not done for the CUSTOMERS table when schema stats are gathered.
B. Statistics collection is not done for the CUSTOMERS table when database stats are gathered.
C. Any existing statistics for the CUSTOMERS table are still available to the optimizer at parse time.
D. Statistics gathered on the CUSTOMERS table when schema stats are gathered are stored as pending statistics.
E. Statistics gathered on the CUSTOMERS table when database stats are gathered are stored as pending statistics.

Correct Answer: CDE

Explanation/Reference:

* SET_TABLE_PREFS Procedure

This procedure is used to set the statistics preferences of the specified table in the specified schema.

* Example:

Using Pending Statistics

Assume many modifications have been made to the employees table since the last time statistics were gathered. To ensure that the cost-based optimizer is still picking the best plan, statistics should be gathered once again; however, the user is concerned that new statistics will cause the optimizer to choose bad plans when the current ones are acceptable. The user can do the following:

EXEC DBMS_STATS.SET_TABLE_PREFS('hr', 'employees', 'PUBLISH', 'false');

By setting the employees tables publish preference to FALSE, any statistics gather from now on will not be automatically published. The newly gathered statistics will be marked as pending.

QUESTION 17

Examine the following impdp command to import a database over the network from a pre-12c Oracle database (source):

```
$>  impdp <user_name> full=Y network_link=hrdb_test transportable=always
    transport_datafiles=
        '/u01/app/oracle/oradata/hrdb/sales01.dbf',
        '/u01/app/oracle/oradata/hrdb/cust01.dbf',
        '/u01/app/oracle/oradata/hrdb/emp01.dbf',
    version=12 logfile=import.log
```

Which three are prerequisites for successful execution of the command? (Choose three.)

A. The import operation must be performed by a user on the target database by a user with the DATAPUMP_IMP_FULL_DATABASE role, and the database link must connect to a user with the DATAPUMP_EXP_FULL_DATABASE role on the source database.

B. All the user-defined tablespaces must be in read-only mode on the source database.

C. The export dump file must be created before starting the import on the target database.

D. The source and target database must be running on the same operating system (OS) with the same endianness.

E. The impdp operation must be performed by the same user that performed the expdp operation.

Correct Answer: ABD

Explanation/Reference:

In this case we have run the impdp without performing any conversion if endian format is different then we have to first perform conversion.

QUESTION 18

Which two are true concerning a multitenant container database with three pluggable database? (Choose two.)

A. All administration tasks must be done to a specific pluggable database.
B. The pluggable databases increase patching time.
C. The pluggable databases reduce administration effort.
D. The pluggable databases are patched together.
E. Pluggable databases are only used for database consolidation.

Correct Answer: CD

QUESTION 19

Examine the current value for the following parameters in your database instance:

SGA_MAX_SIZE = 1024M SGA_TARGET = 700M DB_8K_CACHE_SIZE = 124M LOG_BUFFER = 200M

You issue the following command to increase the value of DB_8K_CACHE_SIZE: SQL> ALTER SYSTEM SET DB_8K_CACHE_SIZE=140M;
Which statement is true?

A. It fails because the DB_8K_CACHE_SIZE parameter cannot be changed dynamically.
B. It succeeds only if memory is available from the autotuned components if SGA.
C. It fails because an increase in DB_8K_CACHE_SIZE cannot be accommodated within SGA_TARGET.
D. It fails because an increase in DB_8K_CACHE_SIZE cannot be accommodated within SGA_MAX_SIZE.

Correct Answer: D

Explanation/Reference:

* The SGA_TARGET parameter can be dynamically increased up to the value specified for the SGA_MAX_SIZE parameter, and it can also be reduced.

* Example:

suppose you have an environment with the following configuration:

SGA_MAX_SIZE = 1024M SGA_TARGET = 512M DB_8K_CACHE_SIZE = 128M

In this example, the value of SGA_TARGET can be resized up to 1024M and can also be reduced until one or more of the automatically sized components reaches its minimum size. The exact value depends on environmental factors such as the number of CPUs on the system. However, the value of DB_8K_CACHE_SIZE remains fixed at all times at 128M

* DB_8K_CACHE_SIZE
Size of cache for 8K buffers

* For example, consider this configuration:

SGA_TARGET = 512M DB_8K_CACHE_SIZE = 128M
In this example, increasing DB_8K_CACHE_SIZE by 16 M to 144M means that the 16M is taken away from the automatically sized components. Likewise, reducing DB_8K_CACHE_SIZE by 16M to 112M means that the 16M is given to the automatically sized components.

QUESTION 20

Which three statements are true concerning unplugging a pluggable database (PDB)? (Choose three.)

A. The PDB must be open in read only mode.
B. The PDB must be dosed.
C. The unplugged PDB becomes a non-CDB.
D. The unplugged PDB can be plugged into the same multitenant container database (CDB)
E. The unplugged PDB can be plugged into another CDB.
F. The PDB data files are automatically removed from disk.

Correct Answer:

Explanation/Reference:

B, not A: The PDB must be closed before unplugging it.

D: An unplugged PDB contains data dictionary tables, and some of the columns in these encode information in an endianness-sensitive way. There is no supported way to handle the conversion of such columns automatically. This means, quite simply, that an unplugged PDB cannot be moved across an endianness difference.

E (not F): To exploit the new unplug/plug paradigm for patching the Oracle version most effectively, the source and destination CDBs should share a filesystem so that the PDB's datafiles can remain in place.

QUESTION 21

You wish to enable an audit policy for all database users, except SYS, SYSTEM, and SCOTT. You issue the following statements:
SQL> AUDIT POLICY ORA_DATABASE_PARAMETER EXCEPT SYS;
SQL> AUDIT POLICY ORA_DATABASE_PARAMETER EXCEPT SYSTEM; SQL> AUDIT POLICY ORA_DATABASE_PARAMETER EXCEPT SCOTT;

For which database users is the audit policy now active?

A. All users except SYS
B. All users except SCOTT
C. All users except sys and SCOTT

D. All users except sys, system, and SCOTT

Correct Answer: B

Explanation/Reference:

If you run multiple AUDIT statements on the same unified audit policy but
specify different EXCEPT users, then Oracle Database uses the last
exception user list, not any of the users from the preceding lists. This
means the effect of the earlier AUDIT POLICY ... EXCEPT statements are
overridden by the latest AUDIT POLICY ... EXCEPT statement.

Note:
* The ORA_DATABASE_PARAMETER policy audits commonly used
   Oracle Database parameter settings. By default, this policy is not enabled.
* You can use the keyword ALL to audit all actions. The following example
shows how to audit all actions on the HR.EMPLOYEES table, except
actions by user pmulligan.

Example Auditing All Actions on a Table

CREATE AUDIT POLICY all_actions_on_hr_emp_pol ACTIONS ALL ON
HR.EMPLOYEES;

AUDIT POLICY all_actions_on_hr_emp_pol EXCEPT pmulligan;

QUESTION 22

On your Oracle 12c database, you invoked SQL *Loader to load data into
the EMPLOYEES table in the HR schema by issuing the following
command:

$> sqlldr hr/hr@pdb table=employees

Which two statements are true regarding the command? (Choose two.)

A. It succeeds with default settings if the EMPLOYEES table belonging to
    HR is already defined in the database.
B. It fails because no SQL *Loader data file location is specified.
C. It fails if the HR user does not have the CREATE ANY DIRECTORY
    privilege.
D. It fails because no SQL *Loader control file location is specified.

Correct Answer: AC

Explanation/Reference:

Note:

* SQL*Loader is invoked when you specify the sqlldr command and, optionally, parameters that establish session characteristics.

QUESTION 23

After implementing full Oracle Data Redaction, you change the default value for the NUMBER data type as follows:

```
SQL> SELECT NUMBER_VALUE FROM REDACTION_VALUES_FOR_TYPE_FULL;

NUMBER_VALUE
------------
           0

SQL> EXEC DBMS_REDACT.UPDATE_FULL_REDACTION_VALUES(-1)

PL/SQL procedure successfully completed.

SQL> select number_value from redaction_values_for_type_full;

NUMBER_VALUE
------------
          -1
```

After changing the value, you notice that FULL redaction continues to redact numeric data with zero. What must you do to activate the new default value for numeric full redaction?

A. Re-enable redaction policies that use FULL data redaction.
B. Re-create redaction policies that use FULL data redaction.
C. Re-connect the sessions that access objects with redaction policies defined on them.
D. Flush the shared pool.
E. Restart the database instance.

Correct Answer: E

Explanation/Reference:

About Altering the Default Full Data Redaction Value
You can alter the default displayed values for full Data Redaction polices. By default, 0 is the redacted value when Oracle Database performs full

redaction (DBMS_REDACT.FULL) on a column of the NUMBER data type.
If you want to change it to another value (for example, 7), then you can run
the DBMS_REDACT.UPDATE_FULL_REDACTION_VALUES procedure
to modify this value. The modification applies to all of the Data Redaction
policies in the current database instance. After you modify a value, you
must restart the database for it to take effect.

Note:
* The DBMS_REDACT package provides an interface to Oracle Data
Redaction, which enables you to mask (redact) data that is returned from
queries issued by low-privileged users or an application.
* UPDATE_FULL_REDACTION_VALUES Procedure

This procedure modifies the default displayed values for a Data Redaction
policy for full redaction.

* After you create the Data Redaction policy, it is automatically enabled and
  ready to redact data.

* Oracle Data Redaction enables you to mask (redact) data that is returned
from queries issued by low-privileged users or applications. You can redact
column data by using one of the following methods:

/ Full redaction.
/ Partial redaction.
/ Regular expressions.
/ Random redaction.
/ No redaction.

QUESTION 24

You must track all transactions that modify certain tables in the sales
schema for at least three years. Automatic undo management is enabled
for the database with a retention of one day.
Which two must you do to track the transactions? (Choose two.)

A. Enable supplemental logging for the database.
B. Specify undo retention guarantee for the database.
C. Create a Flashback Data Archive in the tablespace where the tables
    are stored.
D. Create a Flashback Data Archive in any suitable tablespace.
E. Enable Flashback Data Archiving for the tables that require tracking.

Correct Answer: DE

Explanation/Reference:

E: By default, flashback archiving is disabled for any table. You can enable flashback archiving for a table if you have the FLASHBACK ARCHIVE object privilege on the Flashback Data Archive that you want to use for that table.
D: Creating a Flashback Data Archive

/ Create a Flashback Data Archive with the CREATE FLASHBACK ARCHIVE statement, specifying the following:

Name of the Flashback Data Archive

Name of the first tablespace of the Flashback Data Archive

(Optional) Maximum amount of space that the Flashback Data Archive can use in the first tablespace

/ Create a Flashback Data Archive named fla2 that uses tablespace tbs2, whose data will be retained for two years: CREATE FLASHBACK ARCHIVE fla2 TABLESPACE tbs2 RETENTION 2 YEAR;

QUESTION 25

You are the DBA supporting an Oracle 11g Release 2 database and wish to move a table containing several DATE, CHAR, VARCHAR2, and NUMBER data types, and the table's indexes, to another tablespace.

The table does not have a primary key and is used by an OLTP application.

Which technique will move the table and indexes while maintaining the highest level of availability to the application?

A. Oracle Data Pump.
B. An ALTER TABLE MOVE to move the table and ALTER INDEX REBUILD to move the indexes.
C. An ALTER TABLE MOVE to move the table and ALTER INDEX REBUILD ONLINE to move the indexes.
D. Online Table Redefinition.
E. Edition-Based Table Redefinition.

Correct Answer: D

Explanation:

* Oracle Database provides a mechanism to make table structure modifications without significantly affecting the availability of the table. The mechanism is called online table redefinition. Redefining tables online provides a substantial increase in availability compared to traditional methods of redefining tables.

* To redefine a table online:

Choose the redefinition method: by key or by rowid

* By key—Select a primary key or pseudo-primary key to use for the redefinition. Pseudo-primary keys are unique keys with all component columns having NOT NULL constraints. For this method, the versions of the tables before and after redefinition should have the same primary key columns. This is the preferred and default method of redefinition.

* By rowid—Use this method if no key is available. In this method, a hidden column named M_ROW$$ is added to the post-redefined version of the table. It is recommended that this column be dropped or marked as unused after the redefinition is complete. If COMPATIBLE is set to 10.2.0 or higher, the final phase of redefinition automatically sets this column unused. You can then use the ALTER TABLE ... DROP UNUSED COLUMNS statement to drop it.

You cannot use this method on index-organized tables.

Note:

* When you rebuild an index, you use an existing index as the data source. Creating an index in this manner enables you to change storage characteristics or move to a new tablespace. Rebuilding an index based on an existing data source removes intra-block fragmentation. Compared to dropping the index and using the CREATE INDEX statement, re-creating an existing index offers better performance.

Incorrect:

Not E: Edition-based redefinition enables you to upgrade the database component of an application while it is in use, thereby minimizing or eliminating down time.

QUESTION 26

To implement Automatic Management (AMM), you set the following parameters:

```
MEMORY_MAX_TARGET=600M
SGA_MAX_SIZE=500M
MEMORY_TARGET=600M
OPEN_CURSORS=300
SGA_TARGET=300M
PROCESSES=150
STATISTICS_LEVEL=BASIC
PGA_AGGREGATE_TARGET=0
```

When you try to start the database instance with these parameter settings, you receive the following error message:

SQL > startup
ORA-00824: cannot set SGA_TARGET or MEMORY_TARGET due to existing internal settings, see alert log for more information. Identify the reason the instance failed to start.

A. The PGA_AGGREGATE_TARGET parameter is set to zero.
B. The STATISTICS_LEVEL parameter is set to BASIC.
C. Both the SGA_TARGET and MEMORY_TARGET parameters are set.
D. The SGA_MAX_SIZE and SGA_TARGET parameter values are not equal.

Correct Answer: B

Explanation/Reference:

Example:
SQL> startup force
ORA-00824: cannot set SGA_TARGET or MEMORY_TARGET due to existing internal settings
ORA-00848: STATISTICS_LEVEL cannot be set to BASIC with SGA_TARGET or MEMORY_TARGET

QUESTION 27

You upgrade your Oracle database in a multiprocessor environment. As a recommended you execute the following script: SQL > @utlrp.sql

Which two actions does the script perform? (Choose two.)

A. Parallel compilation of only the stored PL/SQL code
B. Sequential recompilation of only the stored PL/SQL code
C. Parallel recompilation of any stored PL/SQL code
D. Sequential recompilation of any stored PL/SQL code
E. Parallel recompilation of Java code
F. Sequential recompilation of Java code

Correct Answer: CE

Explanation/Reference:

utlrp.sql and utlprp.sql

The utlrp.sql and utlprp.sql scripts are provided by Oracle to recompile all invalid objects in the database. They are typically run after major database changes such as upgrades or patches. They are located in the $ORACLE_HOME/rdbms/admin directory and provide a wrapper on the UTL_RECOMP package. The utlrp.sql script simply calls the utlprp.sql script with a command line parameter of "0". The utlprp.sql accepts a single integer parameter that indicates the level of parallelism as follows.

0 - The level of parallelism is derived based on the CPU_COUNT parameter. 1 - The recompilation is run serially, one object at a time. N - The recompilation is run in parallel with "N" number of threads. Both scripts must be run as the SYS user, or another user with SYSDBA, to work correctly.

QUESTION 28

Which two statements are true concerning dropping a pluggable database (PDB)? (Choose two.)

A. The PDB must be open in read-only mode.
B. The PDB must be in mount state.
C. The PDB must be unplugged.
D. The PDB data files are always removed from disk.

E. A dropped PDB can never be plugged back into a multitenant container database (CDB).

Correct Answer: BC

Explanation/Reference:

http://docs.oracle.com/database/121/ADMIN/cdb_plug.htm#ADMIN13658

QUESTION 29

You notice a performance change in your production Oracle 12c database. You want to know which change caused this performance difference. Which method or feature should you use?

A. Compare Period ADDM report
B. AWR Compare Period report
C. Active Session History (ASH) report
D. Taking a new snapshot and comparing it with a preserved snapshot

Correct Answer: A

QUESTION 30

You want to capture column group usage and gather extended statistics for better cardinality estimates for the CUSTOMERS table in the SH schema.

Examine the following steps:
1. Issue the SELECT DBMS_STATS.CREATE_EXTENDED_STATS ('SH', 'CUSTOMERS') FROM dual statement.
2. Execute the DBMS_STATS.SEED_COL_USAGE (null, 'SH', 500) procedure.
3. Execute the required queries on the CUSTOMERS table.
4. Issue the SELECT DBMS_STATS.REPORT_COL_USAGE ('SH', 'CUSTOMERS') FROM dual statement.
Identify the correct sequence of steps. A. 3, 2, 1, 4
B. 2, 3, 4, 1
C. 4, 1, 3, 2
D. 3, 2, 4, 1

Correct Answer: B

Explanation/Reference:

Step 1 (2). Seed column usage
Oracle must observe a representative workload, in order to determine the appropriate column groups. Using the new procedure DBMS_STATS.SEED_COL_USAGE, you tell Oracle how long it should observe the workload.
Step 2: (3) You don't need to execute all of the queries in your work during this window. You can simply run explain plan for some of your longer running queries to ensure column group information is recorded for these queries.
Step 3. (1) Create the column groups
At this point you can get Oracle to automatically create the column groups for each of the tables based on the usage information captured during the monitoring window. You simply have to call the DBMS_STATS.CREATE_EXTENDED_STATS function for each table.This function requires just two arguments, the schema name and the table name. From then on, statistics will be maintained for each column group whenever statistics are gathered on the table.

Note:
* DBMS_STATS.REPORT_COL_USAGE reports column usage information and records all the SQL operations the database has processed for a given object.

* The Oracle SQL optimizer has always been ignorant of the implied relationships between data columns within the same table. While the optimizer has traditionally analyzed the distribution of values within a column, he does not collect value-based relationships between columns.
* Creating extended statisticsHere are the steps to create extended statistics for related table columns
withdbms_stats.created_extended_stats:
1 - The first step is to create column histograms for the related columns.2 – Next, we run dbms_stats.create_extended_stats to relate the columns together. Unlike a traditional procedure that is invoked via an execute ("exec") statement, Oracle extended statistics are created via a select statement.

QUESTION 31

An application accesses a small lookup table frequently. You notice that the required data blocks are getting aged out of the default buffer cache. How would you guarantee that the blocks for the table never age out?

A. Configure the KEEP buffer pool and alter the table with the corresponding storage clause.
B. Increase the database buffer cache size.
C. Configure the RECYCLE buffer pool and alter the table with the corresponding storage clause.
D. Configure Automata Shared Memory Management.
E. Configure Automatic Memory Management.

Correct Answer: A

Explanation/Reference:

Schema objects are referenced with varying usage patterns; therefore, their cache behavior may be quite different. Multiple buffer pools enable you to address these differences. You can use a KEEP buffer pool to maintain objects in the buffer cache and a RECYCLE buffer pool to prevent objects from consuming unnecessary space in the cache. When an object is allocated to a cache, all blocks from that object are placed in that cache. Oracle maintains a DEFAULT buffer pool for objects that have not been assigned to one of the buffer pools.

QUESTION 32

You conned using SQL Plus to the root container of a multitenant container database (CDB) with SYSDBA privilege. The CDB has several pluggable databases (PDBs) open in the read/write mode.
There are ongoing transactions in both the CDB and PDBs.

What happens alter issuing the SHUTDOWN TRANSACTIONAL statement?

A. The shutdown proceeds immediately. The shutdown proceeds as soon as all transactions in the PDBs are either committed or rolled hack.
B. The shutdown proceeds as soon as all transactions in the CDB are either committed or rolled back.
C. The shutdown proceeds as soon as all transactions in both the CDB and PDBs are either committed or rolled back.
D. The statement results in an error because there are open PDBs.

Correct Answer: B

Explanation/Reference:

* SHUTDOWN [ABORT | IMMEDIATE | NORMAL | TRANSACTIONAL
  [LOCAL]]

Shuts down a currently running Oracle Database instance, optionally closing and dismounting a database. If the current database is a pluggable database, only the pluggable database is closed. The consolidated instance continues to run.

Shutdown commands that wait for current calls to complete or users to disconnect such as SHUTDOWN NORMAL and SHUTDOWN TRANSACTIONAL have a time limit that the SHUTDOWN command will wait. If all events blocking the shutdown have not occurred within the time limit, the shutdown command cancels with the following message:

ORA-01013: user requested cancel of current operation

* If logged into a CDB, shutdown closes the CDB instance.

To shutdown a CDB or non CDB, you must be connected to the CDB or non CDB instance that you want to close, and then enter SHUTDOWN Database closed. Database dismounted. Oracle instance shut down.
To shutdown a PDB, you must log into the PDB to issue the SHUTDOWN command. SHUTDOWN Pluggable Database closed.

Note:

* Prerequisites for PDB Shutdown

When the current container is a pluggable database (PDB), the SHUTDOWN command can only be used if:

The current user has SYSDBA, SYSOPER, SYSBACKUP, or SYSDG system privilege. The privilege is either commonly granted or locally granted in the PDB.
The current user exercises the privilege using AS SYSDBA, AS SYSOPER, AS SYSBACKUP, or AS SYSDG at connect time. To close a PDB, the PDB must be open.

QUESTION 33

Your database supports an online transaction processing (OLTP) application. The application is undergoing some major schema changes, such as addition of new indexes and materialized views. You want to check the impact of these changes on workload performance.

What should you use to achieve this?

A. Database replay
B. SQL Tuning Advisor
C. SQL Access Advisor
D. SQL Performance Analyzer
E. Automatic Workload Repository compare reports

Correct Answer: D

Explanation/Reference:

You can use the SQL Performance Analyzer to analyze the SQL performance impact of any type of system change. Examples of common system changes include:

• Database upgrades
• Configuration changes to the operating system, hardware, or database
• Database initialization parameter changes
• Schema changes, such as adding new indexes or materialized views
• Gathering optimizer statistics
• SQL tuning actions, such as creating SQL profiles

http://docs.oracle.com/cd/B28359_01/server.111/b28318/intro.htm#CNCPT 961

QUESTION 34

An administrator account is granted the CREATE SESSION and SET CONTAINER system privileges. A multitenant container database (CDB) instant has the following parameter set:
THREADED_EXECUTION = FALSE

Which four statements are true about this administrator establishing connections to root in a CDB that has been opened in read only mode? (Choose four.)

A. You can connect as a common user by using the connect statement.
B. You can connect as a local user by using the connect statement.
C. You can connect by using easy connect.
D. You can connect by using OS authentication.
E. You can connect by using a Net Service name.
F. You can connect as a local user by using the SET CONTAINER statement.

Correct Answer: ACDE

QUESTION 35

You notice a performance change in your production Oracle database and you want to know which change has made this performance difference. You generate the Compare Period Automatic Database Diagnostic Monitor (ADDM) report to further investigation.

Which three findings would you get from the report? (Choose three.)

A. It detects any configuration change that caused a performance difference in both time periods.

B. It identifies any workload change that caused a performance difference in both time periods.

C. It detects the top wait events causing performance degradation.

D. It shows the resource usage for CPU, memory, and I/O in both time periods.

E. It shows the difference in the size of memory pools in both time periods.

F. It gives information about statistics collection in both time periods.

Correct Answer: ABD

Explanation/Reference:

Keyword: shows the difference.

* Full ADDM analysis across two AWR snapshot periods Detects causes, measure effects, then correlates them Causes: workload changes, configuration changes
Effects: regressed SQL, reach resource limits (CPU, I/O, memory, interconnect) Makes actionable recommendations along with quantified impact

* Identify what changed
/ Configuration changes, workload changes

* Performance degradation of the database occurs when your database was performing optimally in the past, such as 6 months ago, but has gradually degraded to a point where it becomes noticeable to the users. The Automatic Workload Repository (AWR) Compare Periods report enables you to compare database performance between two periods of time.

While an AWR report shows AWR data between two snapshots (or two points in time), the AWR Compare Periods report shows the difference (ABE) between two periods (or two AWR reports with a total of four snapshots). Using the AWR Compare Periods report helps you to identify detailed performance attributes and configuration settings that differ between two time periods.

QUESTION 36

Which three statements are true about adaptive SQL plan management? (Choose three.)

A. It automatically performs verification or evolves non-accepted plans, in COMPREHENSIVE mode when they perform better than existing accepted plans.
B. The optimizer always uses the fixed plan, if the fixed plan exists in the plan baseline.
C. It adds new, bettor plans automatically as fixed plans to the baseline.
D. The non-accepted plans are automatically accepted and become usable by the optimizer if they perform better than the existing accepted plans.
E. The non-accepted plans in a SQL plan baseline are automatically evolved, in COMPREHENSIVE mode, during the nightly maintenance window and a persistent verification report is generated.

Correct Answer: ADE

Explanation/Reference:

With adaptive SQL plan management, DBAs no longer have to manually run the verification or evolve process for non-accepted plans. When automatic SQL tuning is in COMPREHENSIVE mode, it runs a verification or evolve process for all SQL statements that have non-accepted plans during the nightly maintenance window. If the non-accepted plan performs better than the existing accepted plan (or plans) in the SQL plan baseline, then the plan is automatically accepted and becomes usable by the optimizer. After the verification is complete, a persistent report is generated detailing how the non-accepted plan performs compared to the accepted plan performance. Because the evolve process is now an AUTOTASK, DBAs can also schedule their own evolve job at end time.

Note:

* The optimizer is able to adapt plans on the fly by predetermining multiple subplans for portions of the plan.

* Adaptive plans, introduced in Oracle Database 12c, enable the optimizer to defer the final plan decision for a statement until execution time. The optimizer instruments its chosen plan (the default plan) with statistics collectors so that it can detect at runtime, if its cardinality estimates differ greatly from the actual number of rows seen by the operations in the plan. If there is a significant difference, then the plan or a portion of it will be automatically adapted to avoid suboptimal performance on the first execution of a SQL statement.

QUESTION 37

You executed a DROP USER CASCADE on an Oracle 11g release 1 database and immediately realized that you forgot to copy the OCA.EXAM_RESULTS table to the OCP schema.

The RECYCLE_BIN enabled before the DROP USER was executed and the OCP user has been granted the FLASHBACK ANY TABLE system privilege. What is the quickest way to recover the contents of the OCA.EXAM_RESULTS table to the OCP schema?

A. Execute FLASHBACK TABLE OCA.EXAM_RESULTS TO BEFORE DROP RENAME TO OCP.EXAM_RESULTS; connected as SYSTEM.
B. Recover the table using traditional Tablespace Point In Time Recovery.
C. Recover the table using Automated Tablespace Point In Time Recovery.
D. Recovery the table using Database Point In Time Recovery.
E. Execute FLASHBACK TABLE OCA.EXAM_RESULTS TO BEFORE DROP RENAME TO EXAM_RESULTS; connected as the OCP user.

Correct Answer: C

Explanation/Reference:

RMAN tablespace point-in-time recovery (TSPITR).

Recovery Manager (RMAN) TSPITR enables quick recovery of one or more tablespaces in a database to an earlier time without affecting the rest of the tablespaces and objects in the database.

Fully Automated (the default)

In this mode, RMAN manages the entire TSPITR process including the auxiliary instance. You specify the tablespaces of the recovery set, an auxiliary destination, the target time, and you allow RMAN to manage all other aspects of TSPITR.

The default mode is recommended unless you specifically need more control over the location of recovery set files after TSPITR, auxiliary set files during TSPITR, channel settings and parameters or some other aspect of your auxiliary instance.

QUESTION 38

You created a new database using the "create database" statement without specifying the "ENABLE PLUGGABLE" clause. What are two effects of not using the "ENABLE PLUGGABLE database" clause?

A. The database is created as a non-CDB and can never contain a PDB.
B. The database is treated as a PDB and must be plugged into an existing multitenant container database (CDB).
C. The database is created as a non-CDB and can never be plugged into a CDB.
D. The database is created as a non-CDB but can be plugged into an existing CDB.
E. The database is created as a non-CDB but will become a CDB whenever the first PDB is plugged in.

Correct Answer: AD

Explanation/Reference:

A (not B,not E): The CREATE DATABASE ... ENABLE PLUGGABLE DATABASE SQL statement creates a new CDB. If you do not specify the ENABLE PLUGGABLE DATABASE clause, then the newly created database is a non-CDB and can never contain PDBs.

D: You can create a PDB by plugging in a Non-CDB as a PDB. The following graphic depicts the options for creating a PDB:

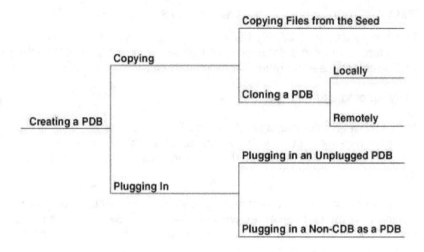

Incorrect:
Not E: For the duration of its existence, a database is either a CDB or a non-CDB. You cannot transform a non-CDB into a CDB or vice versa. You must define a database as a CDB at creation, and then create PDBs within this CDB.

QUESTION 39

What is the effect of specifying the "ENABLE PLUGGABLE DATABASE" clause in a "CREATE DATABASE" statement?

A. It will create a multitenant container database (CDB) with only the root opened.
B. It will create a CDB with root opened and seed read only.
C. It will create a CDB with root and seed opened and one PDB mounted.
D. It will create a CDB that must be plugged into an existing CDB.
E. It will create a CDB with root opened and seed mounted.

Correct Answer: B

Explanation/Reference:

* The CREATE DATABASE ... ENABLE PLUGGABLE DATABASE SQL statement creates a new CDB. If you do not specify the ENABLE PLUGGABLE DATABASE clause, then the newly created database is a non-CDB and can never contain PDBs.

Along with the root (CDB$ROOT), Oracle Database automatically creates a seed PDB (PDB$SEED). The following graphic shows a newly created CDB:

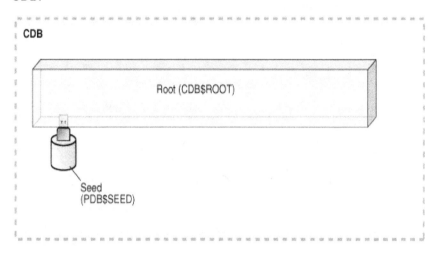

* Creating a PDB

Rather than constructing the data dictionary tables that define an empty PDB from scratch, and then populating its Obj$ and Dependency$ tables, the empty PDB is created when the CDB is created. (Here, we use empty to mean containing no customer-created artifacts.) It is referred to as the seed PDB and has the name PDB$Seed. Every CDB non-negotiably contains a seed PDB; it is non-negotiably always open in read-only mode. This has no conceptual significance; rather, it is just an optimization device. The create PDB operation is implemented as a special case of the clone PDB operation.

QUESTION 40

Examine the following parameters for a database instance:

MEMORY_MAX_TARGET=0 MEMORY_TARGET=0 SGA_TARGET=0 PGA_AGGREGATE_TARGET=500m

Which three initialization parameters are not controlled by Automatic Shared Memory Management (ASMM)? (Choose three.)

A. LOG_BUFFER
B. SORT_AREA_SIZE
C. JAVA_POOL_SIZE
D. STREAMS_POOL_SIZE
E. DB_16K_CACHE_SZIE
F. DB_KEEP_CACHE_SIZE

Correct Answer: AEF

Explanation/Reference:

Manually Sized SGA Components that Use SGA_TARGET Space SGA Component, Initialization Parameter
/ The log buffer LOG_BUFFER
/ The keep and recycle buffer caches DB_KEEP_CACHE_SIZE DB_RECYCLE_CACHE_SIZE
/ Nonstandard block size buffer caches DB_nK_CACHE_SIZE

Note:
* In addition to setting SGA_TARGET to a nonzero value, you must set to zero all initialization parameters listed in the table below to enable full automatic tuning of the automatically sized SGA components.
* Table, Automatically Sized SGA Components and Corresponding Parameters

SGA Component	Initialization Parameter
Fixed SGA and other internal allocations needed by the Oracle Database instance	N/A
The shared pool	SHARED_POOL_SIZE
The large pool	LARGE_POOL_SIZE
The Java pool	JAVA_POOL_SIZE
The buffer cache	DB_CACHE_SIZE
The Streams pool	STREAMS_POOL_SIZE

QUESTION 41

In your multitenant container database (CDB) containing pluggable database (PDBs), you granted the CREATE TABLE privilege to the common user C # # A_ADMIN in root and all PDBs. You execute the following command from the root container:

SQL > REVOKE create table FROM C # # A_ADMIN; What is the result?

A. It executes successfully and the CREATE TABLE privilege is revoked from C # # A_ADMIN in root only.
B. It fails and reports an error because the CONTAINER=ALL clause is not used.
C. It excludes successfully and the CREATE TABLE privilege is revoked from C # # A_ADMIN in root and all PDBs.
D. It fails and reports an error because the CONTAINER=CURRENT clause is not used.
E. It executes successfully and the CREATE TABLE privilege is revoked from C # # A_ADMIN in all PDBs.

Correct Answer: A

Explanation/Reference:

REVOKE ..FROM

If the current container is the root:

/ Specify CONTAINER = CURRENT to revoke a locally granted system privilege, object privilege, or role from a common user or common role. The privilege or role is revoked from the user or role only in the root. This clause does not revoke privileges granted with CONTAINER = ALL.

/ Specify CONTAINER = ALL to revoke a commonly granted system privilege, object privilege on a common object, or role from a common user or common role. The privilege or role is revoked from the user or role across the entire CDB. This clause can revoke only a privilege or role granted with CONTAINER = ALL from the specified common user or common role. This clause does not revoke privileges granted locally with CONTAINER = CURRENT. However, any locally granted privileges that depend on the commonly granted privilege being revoked are also revoked.

If you omit this clause, then CONTAINER = CURRENT is the default.

QUESTION 42

Which three statements are true concerning the multitenant architecture? (Choose three.)

A. Each pluggable database (PDB) has its own set of background processes.

B. A PDB can have a private temp tablespace.
C. PDBs can share the sysaux tablespace.
D. Log switches occur only at the multitenant container database (CDB) level.
E. Different PDBs can have different default block sizes.
F. PDBs share a common system tablespace.
G. Instance recovery is always performed at the CDB level.

Correct Answer: BDG

Explanation/Reference:

B:
* A PDB would have its SYSTEM, SYSAUX, TEMP tablespaces. It can also contain other user created tablespaces in it.
* There is one default temporary tablespace for the entire CDB. However, you can create additional temporary tablespaces in individual PDBs. D:
* There is a single redo log and a single control file for an entire CDB
* A log switch is the point at which the database stops writing to one redo log file and begins writing to another. Normally, a log switch occurs when the current redo log file is completely filled and writing must continue to the next redo log file.

G: instance recovery

The automatic application of redo log records to uncommitted data blocks when a database instance is restarted after a failure.

Incorrect:

Not A:

* There is one set of background processes shared by the root and all PDBs.

* High consolidation density. The many pluggable databases in a single container database share its memory and background processes, letting you operate many more pluggable databases on a particular platform than you can single databases that use the old architecture.

Not C:

There is a separate SYSAUX tablespace for the root and for each PDB.
Not F: There is a separate SYSTEM tablespace for the root and for each PDB.

QUESTION 43

You notice that the elapsed time for an important database scheduler Job is unacceptably long. The job belongs to a scheduler job class and window. Which two actions would reduce the job's elapsed time? (Choose two.)

A. Increasing the priority of the job class to which the job belongs
B. Increasing the job's relative priority within the Job class to which it belongs
C. Increasing the resource allocation for the consumer group mapped to the scheduler job's job class within the plan mapped to the scheduler window
D. Moving the job to an existing higher priority scheduler window with the same schedule and duration
E. Increasing the value of the JOB_QUEUE_PROCESSES parameter
F. Increasing the priority of the scheduler window to which the job belongs

Correct Answer: BC

Explanation/Reference:

B: Job priorities are used only to prioritize among jobs in the same class.

Note: Group jobs for prioritization
Within the same job class, you can assign priority values of 1-5 to individual jobs so that if two jobs in the class are scheduled to start at the same time, the one with the higher priority takes precedence. This ensures that you do not have a less important job preventing the timely completion of a more important one.

C: Set resource allocation for member jobs
Job classes provide the link between the Database Resource Manager and the Scheduler, because each job class can specify a resource consumer group as an attribute. Member jobs then belong to the specified consumer group and are assigned resources according to settings in the current resource plan.

QUESTION 44

You plan to migrate your database from a File system to Automata Storage Management (ASM) on same platform. Which two methods or commands would you use to accomplish this task? (Choose two.)

A. RMAN CONVERT command
B. Data Pump Export and import
C. Conventional Export and Import
D. The BACKUP AS COPY DATABASE . . . command of RMAN
E. DBMS_FILE_TRANSFER with transportable tablespace

Correct Answer: AD

Explanation/Reference:

A:
1. Get the list of all datafiles.

Note: RMAN Backup of ASM Storage

There is often a need to move the files from the file system to the ASM
storage and vice versa. This may come in handy when one of the file
systems is corrupted by some means and then the file may need to be
moved to the other file system.

D: Migrating a Database into ASM

* To take advantage of Automatic Storage Management with an existing
database you must migrate that database into ASM. This migration is
performed using Recovery Manager (RMAN) even if you are not using
RMAN for your primary backup and recovery strategy.

* Example:
Back up your database files as copies to the ASM disk group.

BACKUP AS COPY INCREMENTAL LEVEL 0 DATABASE FORMAT
'+DISK' TAG 'ORA_ASM_MIGRATION';

QUESTION 45

You run a script that completes successfully using SQL*Plus that performs
these actions:
1. Creates a multitenant container database (CDB)
2. Plugs in three pluggable databases (PDBs)
3. Shuts down the CDB instance
4. Starts up the CDB instance using STARTUP OPEN READ WRITE

Which two statements are true about the outcome after running the script? (Choose two.)

A. The seed will be in mount state.
B. The seed will be opened read-only.
C. The seed will be opened read/write.
D. The other PDBs will be in mount state.
E. The other PDBs will be opened read-only.
F. The PDBs will be opened read/write.

Correct Answer: BD

Explanation/Reference:

B: The seed is always read-only.

D: Pluggable databases can be started and stopped using SQL*Plus commands or the ALTER PLUGGABLE DATABASE command.

QUESTION 46

Your database is open and the LISTENER listener running. You stopped the wrong listener LISTENER by issuing the following command: 1snrctl > STOP
What happens to the sessions that are presently connected to the database Instance?

A. They are able to perform only queries.
B. They are not affected and continue to function normally.
C. They are terminated and the active transactions are rolled back.
D. They are not allowed to perform any operations until the listener LISTENER is started.

Correct Answer: B

Explanation/Reference:

The listener is used when the connection is established. The immediate impact of stopping the listener will be that no new session can be established from a remote host. Existing sessions are not compromised.

QUESTION 47

You execute the following PL/SQL:

```
BEGIN
DBMS_FGA.add_policy(
object_schema => 'JIM',
object_name => 'PRODUCTS',
policy_name => 'PROD_AUDIT',
audit_condition => 'PRICE > 10000',
audit_column => 'PRICE');
END;
/
```

Which two statements are true? (Choose two.)

A. Fine-Grained Auditing (FGA) is enabled for the PRICE column in the PRODUCTS table for SELECT statements only when a row with PRICE > 10000 is accessed.
B. FGA is enabled for the PRODUCTS.PRICE column and an audit record is written whenever a row with PRICE > 10000 is accessed.
C. FGA is enabled for all DML operations by JIM on the PRODUCTS.PRICE column.
D. FGA is enabled for the PRICE column of the PRODUCTS table and the SQL statements is captured in the FGA audit trial.

Correct Answer: AB

Explanation/Reference:

DBMS_FGA.add_policy

* The DBMS_FGA package provides fine-grained security functions.
* ADD_POLICY Procedure
This procedure creates an audit policy using the supplied predicate as the audit condition. Incorrect:
Not C: object_schema
The schema of the object to be audited. (If NULL, the current log-on user schema is assumed.)

QUESTION 48

You execute the following commands to audit database activities:

SQL > ALTER SYSTEM SET AUDIT_TRIAL=DB, EXTENDED
SCOPE=SPFILE;
SQL > AUDIT SELECT TABLE, INSERT TABLE, DELETE TABLE BY
JOHN By SESSION WHENEVER SUCCESSFUL;

Which statement is true about the audit record that generated when
auditing after instance restarts?

A. One audit record is created for every successful execution of a
   SELECT, INSERT OR DELETE command on a table, and contains the
   SQL text for the SQL Statements.
B. One audit record is created for every successful execution of a
   SELECT, INSERT OR DELETE command, and contains the execution
   plan for the SQL statements.
C. One audit record is created for the whole session if john successfully
   executes a SELECT, INSERT, or DELETE command, and contains the
   execution plan for the SQL statements.
D. One audit record is created for the whole session if JOHN successfully
   executes a select command, and contains the SQL text and bind
   variables used.
E. One audit record is created for the whole session if john successfully
   executes a SELECT, INSERT, or DELETE command on a table, and
   contains the execution plan, SQL text, and bind variables used.

Correct Answer: A

Explanation/Reference:

Note:

* BY SESSION

In earlier releases, BY SESSION caused the database to write a single
record for all SQL statements or operations of the same type executed on
the same schema objects in the same session. Beginning with this release
(11g) of Oracle Database, both BY SESSION and BY ACCESS cause
Oracle Database to write one audit record for each audited statement and
operation.

* BY ACCESS

Specify BY ACCESS if you want Oracle Database to write one record for each audited statement and operation.

 Note:

If you specify either a SQL statement shortcut or a system privilege that audits a data definition language (DDL) statement, then the database always audits by access. In all other cases, the database honors the BY SESSION or BY ACCESS specification.

* For each audited operation, Oracle Database produces an audit record containing this information:

/ The user performing the operation
/ The type of operation
/ The object involved in the operation

/ The date and time of the operation

QUESTION 49

To enable the Database Smart Flash Cache, you configure the following parameters:

DB_FLASH_CACHE_FILE = '/dev/flash_device_1' , '/dev/flash_device_2'
DB_FLASH_CACHE_SIZE=64G

What is the result when you start up the database instance?

A. It results in an error because these parameter settings are invalid.
B. One 64G flash cache file will be used.
C. Two 64G flash cache files will be used.
D. Two 32G flash cache files will be used.

Correct Answer: A

QUESTION 50

You are administering a database and you receive a requirement to apply the following restrictions:
1. A connection must be terminated after four unsuccessful login attempts by user.

2. A user should not be able to create more than four simultaneous sessions.
3. User session must be terminated after 15 minutes of inactivity.
4. Users must be prompted to change their passwords every 15 days.

How would you accomplish these requirements?

A. by granting a secure application role to the users
B. by creating and assigning a profile to the users and setting the REMOTE_OS_AUTHENT parameter to FALSE
C. By creating and assigning a profile to the users and setting the SEC_MAX_FAILED_LOGIN_ATTEMPTS parameter to 4
D. By Implementing Fine-Grained Auditing (FGA) and setting the REMOTE_LOGIN_PASSWORD_FILE parameter to NONE.
E. By implementing the database resource Manager plan and setting the SEC_MAX_FAILED_LOGIN_ATTEMPTS parameters to 4.

Correct Answer: A

Explanation/Reference:

You can design your applications to automatically grant a role to the user who is trying to log in, provided the user meets criteria that you specify. To do so, you create a secure application role, which is a role that is associated with a PL/SQL procedure (or PL/SQL package that contains multiple procedures). The procedure validates the user: if the user fails the validation, then the user cannot log in. If the user passes the validation, then the procedure grants the user a role so that he or she can use the application. The user has this role only as long as he or she is logged in to the application. When the user logs out, the role is revoked.

Incorrect:

Not B: REMOTE_OS_AUTHENT specifies whether remote clients will be authenticated with the value of the OS_AUTHENT_PREFIX parameter.
Not C, not E: SEC_MAX_FAILED_LOGIN_ATTEMPTS specifies the number of authentication attempts that can be made by a client on a connection to the server process. After the specified number of failure attempts, the connection will be automatically dropped by the server process.

Not D: REMOTE_LOGIN_PASSWORDFILE specifies whether Oracle checks for a password file.

Values: shared One or more databases can use the password file. The password file can contain SYS as well as non-SYS users. Exclusive

The password file can be used by only one database. The password file can contain SYS as well as non-SYS users. None

Oracle ignores any password file. Therefore, privileged users must be authenticated by the operating system.

Note:

The REMOTE_OS_AUTHENT parameter is deprecated. It is retained for backward compatibility only.

QUESTION 51

A senior DBA asked you to execute the following command to improve performance: SQL> ALTER TABLE subscribe log STORAGE (BUFFER_POOL recycle);

You checked the data in the SUBSCRIBE_LOG table and found that it is a large table containing one million rows. What could be a reason for this recommendation?

A. The keep pool is not configured.
B. Automatic Workarea Management is not configured.
C. Automatic Shared Memory Management is not enabled.
D. The data blocks in the SUBSCRIBE_LOG table are rarely accessed.
E. All the queries on the SUBSCRIBE_LOG table are rewritten to a materialized view.

Correct Answer: D

Explanation/Reference:

The most of the rows in SUBSCRIBE_LOG table are accessed once a week.

QUESTION 52

Which three tasks can be automatically performed by the Automatic Data Optimization feature of Information lifecycle Management (ILM)? (Choose three.)

A. Tracking the most recent read time for a table segment in a user tablespace
B. Tracking the most recent write time for a table segment in a user tablespace
C. Tracking insert time by row for table rows
D. Tracking the most recent write time for a table block
E. Tracking the most recent read time for a table segment in the SYSAUX tablespace
F. Tracking the most recent write time for a table segment in the SYSAUX tablespace

Correct Answer: ABD

Explanation/Reference:

Incorrect:

Not E, Not F When Heat Map is enabled, all accesses are tracked by the in-memory activity tracking module. Objects in the SYSTEM and SYSAUX tablespaces are not tracked.

* To implement your ILM strategy, you can use Heat Map in Oracle Database to track data access and modification.
Heat Map provides data access tracking at the segment-level and data modification tracking at the segment and row level.

* To implement your ILM strategy, you can use Heat Map in Oracle Database to track data access and modification. You can also use Automatic Data Optimization (ADO) to automate the compression and movement of data between different tiers of storage within the database.

QUESTION 53

You configure your database Instance to support shared server connections.

Which two memory areas that are part of PGA are stored in SGA instead, for shared server connection? (Choose two.)

A. User session data
B. Stack space
C. Private SQL area

D. Location of the runtime area for DML and DDL Statements

E. Location of a part of the runtime area for SELECT statements

Correct Answer: AC

Explanation/Reference:

A: PGA itself is subdivided. The UGA (User Global Area) contains session state information, including stuff like package-level variables, cursor state, etc. Note that, with shared server, the UGA is in the SGA. It has to be, because shared server means that the session state needs to be accessible to all server processes, as any one of them could be assigned a particular session. However, with dedicated server (which likely what you're using), the UGA is allocated in the PGA.

C: The Location of a private SQL area depends on the type of connection established for a session. If a session is connected through a dedicated server, private SQL areas are located in the server process' PGA. However, if a session is connected through a shared server, part of the private SQL area is kept in the SGA.

Note:

* System global area (SGA)
The SGA is a group of shared memory structures, known as SGA components, that contain data and control information for one Oracle Database instance. The SGA is shared by all server and background processes. Examples of data stored in the SGA include cached data blocks and shared SQL areas.

* Program global area (PGA)

A PGA is a memory region that contains data and control information for a server process. It is nonshared memory created by Oracle Database when a server process is started. Access to the PGA is exclusive to the server process. There is one PGA for each server process. Background processes also allocate their own PGAs. The total memory used by all individual PGAs is known as the total instance PGA memory, and the collection of individual PGAs is referred to as the total instance PGA, or just instance PGA. You use database initialization parameters to set the size of the instance PGA, not individual PGAs.

QUESTION 54

Which two statements are true about Oracle Managed Files (OMF)?
(Choose two.)

A. OMF cannot be used in a database that already has data files created
   with user-specified directions.

B. The file system directions that are specified by OMF parameters are
   created automatically.

C. OMF can be used with ASM disk groups, as well as with raw devices,
   for better file management.

D. OMF automatically creates unique file names for table spaces and
   control files.

E. OMF may affect the location of the redo log files and archived log files.

Correct Answer: DE

Explanation/Reference:

D: The database internally uses standard file system interfaces to create
and delete files as needed for the following database structures:

Tablespaces
Redo log files Control files Archived logs
Block change tracking files Flashback logs
RMAN backups

Note:

* Using Oracle-managed files simplifies the administration of an Oracle
Database. Oracle-managed files eliminate the need for you, the DBA, to
directly manage the operating system files that make up an Oracle
Database. With Oracle-managed files, you specify file system directories in
which the database automatically creates, names, and manages files at the
database object level. For example, you need only specify that you want to
create a tablespace; you do not need to specify the name and path of the
tablespace's datafile with the DATAFILE clause.

http://www.oracle-base.com/articles/9i/oracle-managed-files.php
http://docs.oracle.com/cd/B10500_01/server.920/a96521/omf.htm

QUESTION 55

Identify three scenarios in which you would recommend the use of SQL Performance Analyzer to analyze impact on the performance of SQL statements.

A. Change in the Oracle Database version
B. Change in your network infrastructure
C. Change in the hardware configuration of the database server
D. Migration of database storage from non-ASM to ASM storage
E. Database and operating system upgrade

Correct Answer: ACE

Explanation/Reference:

Oracle 11g/12c makes further use of SQL tuning sets with the SQL Performance Analyzer, which compares the performance of the statements in a tuning set before and after a database change. The database change can be as major or minor as you like, such as:

* (E) Database, operating system, or hardware upgrades.
* (A,C) Database, operating system, or hardware configuration changes.
* Database initialization parameter changes.
* Schema changes, such as adding indexes or materialized views.
* Refreshing optimizer statistics.
* Creating or changing SQL profiles.

QUESTION 56

Which two statements are true about the RMAN validate database command? (Choose two.)

A. It checks the database for intrablock corruptions.
B. It can detect corrupt pfiles.
C. It can detect corrupt spfiles.
D. It checks the database for interblock corruptions.
E. It can detect corrupt block change tracking files.

Correct Answer: AC

Explanation/Reference:

Block corruptions can be divided Into Interblock corruption and intrablock corruption. In intrablock corruption. th« corruption occurs within the block itself and can be either physical or logical corruption. In interblock corruption, the corruption occurs between blocks and can only be logical corruption.

(key word) * The VALIDATE command checks for intrablock corruptions only. Only DBVERIFY and the ANALYZE statement detect Interblock corruption. VALIDATE Command Output ••> List of Control File and SPFILE.
File TYPE >»» SPFILE or Control File.
Status >»» OK if no corruption, or FAILED If block corruption is found.
Blocks Failing »»» The number of blocks that fail the corruption check. These blocks are newly corrupt.
Blocks Examined »»» Total number of blocks in the file.

Oracle' Database Backup and Recovery User's Guide
12c Release 1 (12.1) - 16 Validating Database Files and Backups

QUESTION 57

You are required to migrate your 11.2.0.3 database as a pluggable database (PDB) to a multitenant container database (CDB).

The following are the possible steps to accomplish this task:
1. Place all the user-defined tablespace in read-only mode on the source database.
2. Upgrade the source database to a 12c version.
3. Create a new PDB in the target container database.
4. Perform a full transportable export on the source database with the VERSION parameter set to 12 using the expdp utility.
5. Copy the associated data files and export the dump file to the desired location in the target database.
6. Invoke the Data Pump import utility on the new PDB database as a user with the DATAPUMP_IMP_FULL_DATABASE role and specify the full transportable import options.
7. Synchronize the PDB on the target container database by using the DBMS_PDS.SYNC_ODB function.

Identifythe correct order of the required steps.

A. 2, 1, 3, 4, 5, 6
B. 1, 3, 4, 5, 6, 7

C. 1, 4, 3, 5, 6, 7
D. 2, 1, 3, 4, 5, 6, 7
E. 1, 5, 6, 4, 3, 2

Correct Answer: C

Explanation/Reference:

1. Set user tablespaces in the source database to READ ONLY.
2. From the Oracle Database 11g Release 2 {11.2.0.3) environment, export the metadata and any data residing in administrative tablespaces from the source database using the FULL=Y and TRANSPORTABLE=ALWAYS parameters. Note that the VER$ION=12 parameter is required only when exporting from an Oracle Database llg Release 2 database:
3. Copy the tablespace data files from the source system to the destination system. Note that the log file from the export operation will list the data files required to be moved.
4. Create a COB on the destination system, including a PDB into which you will import the source database.
5. In the Oracle Database 12c environment, connect to the pre-created PDB and import the dump file. The act of importing the dump file will plug the tablespace data files into the destination PDB Oracle White Paper - Upgrading to Oracle Database 12c -August 2013

QUESTION 58

Which two statements are true about the Oracle Direct Network File system (DNFS)? (Choose two.)

A. It utilizes the OS file system cache.
B. A traditional NFS mount is not required when using Direct NFS.
C. Oracle Disk Manager can manage NFS on its own, without using the operating kernel NFS driver.
D. Direct NFS is available only in UNIX platforms.
E. Direct NFS can load-balance I/O traffic across multiple network adapters.

Correct Answer: CE

Explanation/Reference:

E: Performance is improved by load balancing across multiple network interfaces (if available).

Note:

* To enable Direct NFS Client, you must replace the standard Oracle Disk
  Manager (ODM) library with one that supports Direct NFS Client.

Incorrect:

Not A:

Direct NFS Client is capable of performing concurrent direct I/O, which
bypasses any operating system level caches and eliminates any operating
system write-ordering locks

Not B:

* To use Direct NFS Client, the NFS file systems must first be mounted and
  available over regular NFS mounts.
* Oracle Direct NFS (dNFS) is an optimized NFS (Network File System)
  client that provides faster and more scalable access to NFS storage located
  on NAS storage devices (accessible over TCP/IP).
Not D: Direct NFS is provided as part of the database kernel, and is thus
available on all supported database platforms - even those that don't
support NFS natively, like Windows.

Note:

* Oracle Direct NFS (dNFS) is an optimized NFS (Network File System)
  client that provides faster and more scalable access to NFS storage
  located on NAS storage devices (accessible over TCP/IP). Direct NFS is
  built directly into the database kernel - just like ASM which is mainly used
  when using DAS or SAN storage.

* Oracle Direct NFS (dNFS) is an internal I/O layer that provides faster
  access to large NFS files than traditional NFS clients.

QUESTION 59

Which three operations can be performed as multipartition operations in
Oracle? (Choose three.)

A. Merge partitions of a list partitioned table

B. Drop partitions of a list partitioned table
C. Coalesce partitions of a hash-partitioned global index.
D. Move partitions of a range-partitioned table
E. Rename partitions of a range partitioned table
F. Merge partitions of a reference partitioned index

Correct Answer: ABF

Explanation/Reference:

Multipartition maintenance enables adding, dropping, truncate, merge, split operations on multiple partitions. A: Merge Multiple Partitions:
The new "ALTER TABLE ... MERGE PARTITIONS " help merge multiple partitions or subpartitions with a single statement. When merging multiple partitions, local and global index operations and semantics for inheritance of unspecified physical attributes are the same for merging two partitions.

B: Drop Multiple Partitions:

The new "ALTER TABLE ... DROP PARTITIONS " help drop multiple partitions or subpartitions with a single statement. Example:
view plaincopy to clipboardprint?
SQL> ALTER TABLE Tab_tst1 DROP PARTITIONS
Tab_tst1_PART5, Tab_tst1_PART6, Tab_tst1_PART7; Table altered
SQL>
Restrictions :

- You can't drop all partitions of the table.
- If the table has a single partition, you will get the error: ORA-14083: cannot drop the onlypartition of a partitioned.

QUESTION 60

A redaction policy was added to the SAL column of the SCOTT.EMP table:

```
BEGIN
  DBMS_REDACT.ADD_POLICY(
    OBJECT_SCHEMA => 'SCOTT',
    OBJECT_NAME   => 'EMP',
    POLICY_NAME   => 'SCOTT_EMP',
    COLUMN_NAME   => 'SAL',
    EXPRESSION    => 'SYS_CONTEXT("SYS_SESSION_ROLES", "MGR") = "FALSE"');
END;
/
```

All users have their default set of system privileges.

For which three situations will data not be redacted? (Choose three.)

A. SYS sessions, regardless of the roles that are set in the session
B. SYSTEM sessions, regardless of the roles that are set in the session
C. SCOTT sessions, only if the MGR role is set in the session
D. SCOTT sessions, only if the MGR role is granted to SCOTT
E. SCOTT sessions, because he is the owner of the table
F. SYSTEM session, only if the MGR role is set in the session

Correct Answer: ABD

QUESTION 61

What is the result of executing a TRUNCATE TABLE command on a table that has Flashback Archiving enabled?

A. It fails with the ORA-665610 Invalid DDL statement on history-tracked message
B. The rows in the table are truncated without being archived.
C. The rows in the table are archived, and then truncated.
D. The rows in both the table and the archive are truncated.

Correct Answer: C

QUESTION 62

Which three activities are supported by the Data Recovery Advisor? (Choose three.)

A. Advising on block checksum failures
B. Advising on inaccessible control files
C. Advising on inaccessible block change tracking files
D. Advising on empty password files
E. Advising on invalid block header field values

Correct Answer: ABE

Explanation/Reference:

* Data Recovery Advisor can diagnose failures such as the following:

/ (B) Components such as datafiles and control files that are not accessible because they do not exist, do not have the correct access permissions, have been taken offline, and so on

/ (A, E) Physical corruptions such as block checksum failures and invalid block header field values

/ Inconsistencies such as a datafile that is older than other database files

/ I/O failures such as hardware errors, operating system driver failures, and exceeding operating system resource limits (for example, the number of open files)

* The Data Recovery Advisor automatically diagnoses corruption or loss of persistent data on disk, determines the appropriate repair options, and executes repairs at the user's request. This reduces the complexity of recovery process, thereby reducing the Mean Time To Recover (MTTR).

QUESTION 63

You create a table with the PERIOD FOR clause to enable the use of the Temporal Validity feature of Oracle Database 12c. Examine the table definition:

```
create table employees
(empno number, salary number,
deptid number, name varchar2(100),
period for employee_time);
```

Which three statements are true concerning the use of the Valid Time Temporal feature for the EMPLOYEES table? (Choose three.)

A. The valid time columns employee_time_start and employee_time_end are automatically created.
B. The same statement may filter on both transaction time and valid temporal time by using the AS OF TIMESTAMP and PERIOD FOR clauses.

C. The valid time columns are not populated by the Oracle Server automatically.
D. The valid time columns are visible by default when the table is described.
E. Setting the session valid time using DBMS_FLASHBACK_ARCHIVE.ENABLE_AT_VALID_TIME sets the visibility for data manipulation language (DML), data definition language (DDL), and queries performed by the session.

Correct Answer: ABC

QUESTION 64

Which three statements are true regarding the use of the Database Migration Assistant for Unicode (DMU)? (Choose three.)

A. A DBA can check specific tables with the DMU
B. The database to be migrated must be opened read-only.
C. The release of the database to be converted can be any release since 9.2.0.8.
D. The DMU can report columns that are too long in the converted characterset.
E. The DMU can report columns that are not represented in the converted characterset.

Correct Answer: ADE

Explanation/Reference:

A: In certain situations, you may want to exclude selected columns or tables from scanning or conversion steps of the migration process.

D: Exceed column limit
The cell data will not fit into a column after conversion.

E: Need conversion
The cell data needs to be converted, because its binary representation in the target character set is different than the representation in the current character set, but neither length limit issues nor invalid representation issues have been found.

* Oracle Database Migration Assistant for Unicode (DMU) is a unique next-generation migration tool providing an end-to-end solution for migrating your

databases from legacy encodings to Unicode.

Incorrect:

Not C: The release of Oracle Database must be 10.2.0.4, 10.2.0.5, 11.1.0.7, 11.2.0.1, or later.

QUESTION 65

Oracle Grid Infrastructure for a stand-alone server is installed on your production host before installing the Oracle Database server. The database and listener are configured by using Oracle Restart.

Examine the following command and its output:

$ crsctl config has
CRS-4622: Oracle High Availability Services auto start is enabled. What does this imply?
A. When you start an instance on a high with SQL *Plus dependent listeners and ASM disk groups are automatically started.
B. When a database instance is started by using the SRVCTL utility and listener startup fails, the instance is still started.
C. When a database is created by using SQL* Plus, it is automatically added to the Oracle Restart configuration.
D. When you create a database service by modifying the SERVICE_NAMES initialization parameter, it is automatically added to the Oracle Restart configuration.

Correct Answer: B

Explanation/Reference:

About Startup Dependencies
Oracle Restart ensures that Oracle components are started in the proper order, in accordance with component dependencies. For example, if database files are stored in Oracle ASM disk groups, then before starting the database instance, Oracle Restart ensures that the Oracle ASM instance is started and the required disk groups are mounted. Likewise, if a component must be shut down, Oracle Restart ensures that dependent components are cleanly shut down first.

Oracle Restart also manages the weak dependency between database instances and the Oracle Net listener (the listener): When a database instance is started, Oracle Restart attempts to start the listener. If the listener startup fails, then the database is still started. If the listener later fails, Oracle Restart does not shut down and restart any database instances.

http://docs.oracle.com/cd/E16655_01/server.121/e17636/restart.htm#ADMIN12710

QUESTION 66

You performed an incremental level 0 backup of a database:

RMAN > BACKUP INCREMENTAL LEVEL 0 DATABASE;

To enable block change tracking after the incremental level 0 backup, you issued this command:

SQL > ALTER DATABASE ENABLE BLOCK CHANGE TRACKING USING FILE
' /mydir/rman_change_track.f';

To perform an incremental level 1 cumulative backup, you issued this command:

RMAN> BACKUP INCREMENTAL LEVEL 1 CUMULATIVE DATABASE;

Which three statements are true? (Choose three.)

A. Backup change tracking will sometimes reduce I/O performed during cumulative incremental backups.
B. The change tracking file must always be backed up when you perform a full database backup.
C. Block change tracking will always reduce I/O performed during cumulative incremental backups.
D. More than one database block may be read by an incremental backup for a change made to a single block.
E. The incremental level 1 backup that immediately follows the enabling of block change tracking will not read the change tracking file to discover changed blocks.

Correct Answer: ADE

QUESTION 67

Which three resources might be prioritized between competing pluggable
databases when creating a multitenant container database plan (CDB plan)
using Oracle Database Resource Manager? (Choose three.)

A. Maximum Undo per consumer group
B. Maximum Idle time
C. Parallel server limit
D. CPU
E. Exadata I/O
F. Local file system I/O

Correct Answer: CDE

QUESTION 68

You created an encrypted tablespace:

```
SQL> CREATE TABLESPACE securespace
        DATAFILE '/home/user/oradata/secure01.dbf'
        SIZE 150M
        ENCRYPTION USING '3DES168'
        DEFAULT STORAGE (ENCRYPT) ;
```

You then closed the encryption wallet because you were advised that this
is secure.

Later in the day, you attempt to create the EMPLOYEES table in the
SECURESPACE tablespace with the SALT option on the EMPLOYEE
column. Which is true about the result?

A. It creates the table successfully but does not encrypt any inserted data
   in the EMPNAME column because the wallet must be opened to encrypt
   columns with SALT.
B. It generates an error when creating the table because the wallet is
   closed.
C. It creates the table successfully, and encrypts any inserted data in the
   EMPNAME column because the wallet needs to be open only for
   tablespace creation.

D. It generates error when creating the table, because the salt option cannot be used with encrypted tablespaces.

Correct Answer: B

QUESTION 69

Which two statements are true when row archival management is enabled? (Choose two.)

A. The ORA_ARCHIVE_STATE column visibility is controlled by the ROW ARCHIVAL VISIBILITY session parameter.
B. The ORA_ARCHIVE_STATE column is updated manually or by a program that could reference activity tracking columns, to indicate that a row is no longer considered active.
C. The ROW ARCHIVAL VISIBILITY session parameter defaults to active rows only.
D. The ORA_ARCHIVE_STATE column is visible if referenced in the select list of a query.
E. The ORA_ARCHIVE_STATE column is updated automatically by the Oracle Server based on activity tracking columns, to Indicate that a row is no longer considered active.

Correct Answer: CD

QUESTION 70

A warehouse fact table in your Oracle 12c Database is range-partitioned by month and accessed frequently with queries that span multiple partitions The table has a local prefixed, range partitioned index.
Some of these queries access very few rows in some partitions and all the rows in other partitions, but these queries still perform a full scan for all accessed partitions.

This commonly occurs when the range of dates begins at the end of a month or ends close to the start of a month.

You want an execution plan to be generated that uses indexed access when only a few rows are accessed from a segment, while still allowing full scans for segments where many rows are returned.

Which three methods could transparently help to achieve this result? (Choose three.)

A. Using a partial local Index on the warehouse fact table month column with indexing disabled to the table partitions that return most of their rows to the queries.

B. Using a partial local Index on the warehouse fact table month column with indexing disabled for the table partitions that return a few rows to the queries.

C. Using a partitioned view that does a UNION ALL query on the partitions of the warehouse fact table, which retains the existing local partitioned column.

D. Converting the partitioned table to a partitioned view that does a UNION ALL query on the monthly tables, which retains the existing local partitioned column.

E. Using a partial global index on the warehouse fact table month column with indexing disabling for the table partitions that return most of their rows to the queries.

F. Using a partial global index on the warehouse fact table month column with indexing disabled for the table partitions that return a few rows to the queries.

Correct Answer: ACE

Explanation/Reference:

Note:

* Oracle 12c now provides the ability to index a subset of partitions and to exclude the others.

Local and global indexes can now be created on a subset of the partitions of a table. Partial Global indexes provide more flexibility in index creation for partitioned tables. For example, index segments can be omitted for the most recent partitions to ensure maximum data ingest rates without impacting the overall data model and access for the partitioned object.

Partial Global Indexes save space and improve performance during loads and queries. This feature supports global indexes that include or index a certain subset of table partitions or subpartitions, and exclude the others. This operation is supported using a default table indexing property. When a table is created or altered, a default indexing property can be specified for the table or its partitions.

QUESTION 71

You use the segment advisor to help determine objects for which space may be reclaimed.

Which three statements are true about the advisor given by the segment advisor? (Choose three.)

A. It may advise the use of online table redefinition for tables in dictionary managed tablespace.
B. It may advise the use of segment shrink for tables in dictionary managed tablespaces it the no chained rows.
C. It may advise the use of online table redefinition for tables in locally managed tablespaces
D. It will detect and advise about chained rows.
E. It may advise the use of segment shrink for free list managed tables.

Correct Answer: ACD

QUESTION 72

In your multitenant container database (CDB) containing same pluggable databases (PDBs), you execute the following commands in the root container:

```
SQL> CREATE ROLE c##role1;

SQL> GRANT create view, create procedure to c##role1;

SQL> GRANT c##role1 to c##a_admin;
```

Which two statements are true? (Choose two.)

A. The C # # ROLE1 role is created in the root database and all the PDBs.
B. The C # # ROLE1 role is created only in the root database because the container clause is not used.
C. Privileges are granted to the C##A_ADMIN user only in the root database.
D. Privileges are granted to the C##A_ADMIN user in the root database and all PDBs.
E. The statement for granting a role to a user fails because the CONTAINER clause is not used.

Correct Answer: AC

Explanation/Reference:

* You can include the CONTAINER clause in several SQL statements, such as the CREATE USER, ALTER USER, CREATE ROLE, GRANT, REVOKE, and ALTER SYSTEM statements.
* * CREATE ROLE with CONTAINER (optional) clause
/ CONTAINER = ALL
Creates a common role.
/ CONTAINER = CURRENT
Creates a local role in the current PDB.

QUESTION 73

Flashback is enabled for your multitenant container database (CDB), which contains two pluggable database (PDBs). A local user was accidently dropped from one of the PDBs.
You want to flash back the PDB to the time before the local user was dropped. You connect to the CDB and execute the following commands:
SQL > SHUTDOWN IMMEDIATE
SQL > STARTUP MOUNT

SQL > FLASHBACK DATABASE to TIME "TO_DATE ('08/20/12' , 'MM/DD/YY')";

Examine following commands:

1. ALTER PLUGGABLE DATABASE ALL OPEN;
2. ALTER DATABASE OPEN;
3. ALTER DATABASE OPEN RESETLOGS;

Which command or commands should you execute next to allow updates to the flashback back schema?

A. Only 1
B. Only 2
C. Only 3
D. 3 and 1
E. 1 and 2

Correct Answer: D

QUESTION 74

Examine the commands executed to monitor database operations:

$> conn sys oracle/oracle@prod as sysdba SQL > VAR eid NUMBER
SQL > EXEC: eid := DBMS_SQL_MONITOR.BEGIN_OPERATION
('batch_job' , FORCED_TRACKING => 'Y');

Which two statements are true? (Choose two.)

A. Database operations will be monitored only when they consume a
   significant amount of resource.
B. Database operations for all sessions will be monitored.
C. Database operations will be monitored only if the STATISTICS_LEVEL
   parameter is set to TYPICAL and
   CONTROL_MANAGEMENT_PACK_ACCESS is set DIAGNISTIC +
   TUNING.
D. Only DML and DDL statements will be monitored for the session.
E. All subsequent statements in the session will be treated as one
   database operation and will be monitored.

Correct Answer: CE

Explanation/Reference:

C: Setting the CONTROL_MANAGEMENT_PACK_ACCESS initialization
parameter to DIAGNOSTIC+TUNING (default) enables monitoring of
database operations. Real-Time SQL Monitoring is a feature of the Oracle
Database Tuning Pack.

Note:

* The DBMS_SQL_MONITOR package provides information about Real-
  time SQL Monitoring and Real-time Database Operation Monitoring.
*(not B) BEGIN_OPERATION Function
starts a composite database operation in the current session.

/ (E) FORCE_TRACKING - forces the composite database operation to be
tracked when the operation starts. You can also use the string variable 'Y'.

/ (not A) NO_FORCE_TRACKING - the operation will be tracked only when
it has consumed at least 5 seconds of CPU or I/O time. You can also use
the string variable 'N'.

QUESTION 75

Which three statements are true about the working of system privileges in a multitenant control database (CDB) that has pluggable databases (PDBs)? (Choose three.)

A. System privileges apply only to the PDB in which they are used.
B. Local users cannot use local system privileges on the schema of a common user.
C. The granter of system privileges must possess the set container privilege.
D. Common users connected to a PDB can exercise privileges across other PDBs.
E. System privileges with the with grant option container all clause must be granted to a common user before the common user can grant privileges to other users

.

Correct Answer: ACE

Explanation/Reference:

A, Not D: In a CDB, PUBLIC is a common role. In a PDB, privileges granted locally to PUBLIC enable all local and common users to exercise these privileges in this PDB only.

C: A user can only perform common operations on a common role, for example, granting privileges commonly to the role, when the following criteria are met: The user is a common user whose current container is root.

The user has the SET CONTAINER privilege granted commonly, which means that the privilege applies in all containers. The user has privilege controlling the ability to perform the specified operation, and this privilege has been granted commonly Incorrect:
Note:

* Every privilege and role granted to Oracle-supplied users and roles is granted commonly except for system privileges granted to PUBLIC, which are granted locally.

QUESTION 76

You are about to plug a multi-terabyte non-CDB into an existing multitenant container database (CDB) as a pluggable database (PDB). The characteristics of the non-CDB are as follows:
- Version: Oracle Database 12c Releases 1 64-bit
- Character set: WE8ISO8859P15
- National character set: AL16UTF16
- O/S: Oracle Linux6 64-bit

The characteristics of the CDB are as follows:

- Version: Oracle Database 12c Release 1 64-bit
- Character set: AL32UTF8
- O/S: Oracle Linux 6 64-bit

Which technique should you use to minimize down time while plugging this non-CDB into the CDB?

A. Transportable database
B. Transportable tablespace
C. Data Pump full export / import
D. The DBMS_PDB package
E. RMAN

Correct Answer: C

QUESTION 77

Which three statements are true about SQL plan directives? (Choose three.)

A. They are tied to a specific statement or SQL ID.
B. They instruct the maintenance job to collect missing statistics or perform dynamic sampling to generate a more optimal plan.
C. They are used to gather only missing statistics.
D. They are created for a query expression where statistics are missing or the cardinality estimates by the optimizer are incorrect.
E. They instruct the optimizer to create only column group statistics.
F. Improve plan accuracy by persisting both compilation and execution statistics in the SYSAUX tablespace.

Correct Answer: BDF

QUESTION 78

Examine these two statements:

```
SQL> CREATE BIGFILE TABLESPACE MRKT
  2    DATAFILE '/u01/app/oracle/oradata/orcl/mrkt.dbf' size 10M LOGGING
  3    EXTENT MANAGEMENT LOCAL SEGMENT SPACE MANAGEMENT AUTO;

Tablespace created.

SQL> ALTER DATABASE DEFAULT TABLESPACE MRKT;

Database altered.
```

Which three are true about the MRKT tablespace? (Choose three.)

A. The MRKT tablespace is created as a small file tablespace, because the file size is less than the minimum required for big file files.
B. The MRKT tablespace may be dropped if it has no contents.
C. Users who were using the old default tablespace will have their default tablespaces changed to the MRKT tablespace.
D. No more data files can be added to the tablespace.
E. The relative file number of the tablespace is not stored in rowids for the table rows that are stored in the MRKT tablespace.

Correct Answer: CDE

QUESTION 79

In your database, you want to ensure that idle sessions that are blocking active are automatically terminated after a specified period of time. How would you accomplish this?
A. Setting a metric threshold
B. Implementing Database Resource Manager
C. Enabling resumable timeout for user sessions
D. Decreasing the value of the IDLE_TIME resource limit in the default profile

Correct Answer: B

QUESTION 80

You Execute the Following command to create a password file in the database server:

$ orapwd file = '+DATA/PROD/orapwprod entries = 5 ignorecase = N format = 12' Which two statements are true about the password file? (Choose two.)

A. It records the usernames and passwords of users when granted the DBA role.
B. It contains the usernames and passwords of users for whom auditing is enabled.
C. Is used by Oracle to authenticate users for remote database administration.
D. It records the usernames and passwords of all users when they are added to the OSDBA or OSOPER operating system groups.
E. It supports the SYSBACKUP, SYSDG, and SYSKM system privileges.

Correct Answer: CE

QUESTION 81

Identify two situations in which the alert log file is updated.

A. Running a query on a table returns ORA-600: Internal Error.
B. Inserting a value into a table returns ORA-01722: invalid number.
C. Creating a table returns ORA-00955: name us already in used by an existing object.
D. Inserting a value into a table returns ORA-00001: unique constraint (SYS.OK_TECHP) violated.
E. Rebuilding an index using ALTER INDEX . . . REBUILD fails with an ORA-01578: ORACLE data block corrupted (file # 14, block # 50) error.

Correct Answer: AE

Explanation/Reference:

The alert log is a chronological log of messages and errors, and includes the following items:

*All internal errors (ORA-600), block corruption errors (ORA-1578), and deadlock errors (ORA-60) that occur

* Administrative operations, such as CREATE, ALTER, and DROP
  statements and STARTUP, SHUTDOWN, and ARCHIVELOG statements

* Messages and errors relating to the functions of shared server and
  dispatcher processes

* Errors occurring during the automatic refresh of a materialized view

* The values of all initialization parameters that had nondefault values at
  the time the database and instance start

Note:
* The alert log file (also referred to as the ALERT.LOG) is a chronological
log of messages and errors written out by an Oracle Database. Typical
messages found in this file is: database startup, shutdown, log switches,
space errors, etc. This file should constantly be monitored to detect
unexpected messages and corruptions.

QUESTION 82

Examine the query and its output executed In an RDBMS Instance:

```
SQL> SELECT * FROM v$pwfile_users:

USERNAME                                   SYSDB SYSOP SYSAS SYSBA SYSDG SYSKM      CON_ID
----------------------------------------   ----- ----- ----- ----- ----- -----   ------------
SYS                                        TRUE  TRUE  FALSE FALSE FALSE FALSE           0
C##B_ADMIN                                 FALSE FALSE FALSE TRUE  FALSE FALSE           0
C##C_ADMIN                                 FALSE FALSE FALSE FALSE TRUE  FALSE           0
C##A_ADMIN                                 FALSE FALSE FALSE FALSE FALSE TRUE            0
C##D_ADMIN                                 FALSE FALSE TRUE  FALSE FALSE FALSE           0
```

Which three statements are true about the users (other than sys) in the
output? (Choose three.)

A. The C # # B_ADMIN user can perform all backup and recovery
   operations using RMAN only.
B. The C # # C_ADMIN user can perform the data guard operation with
   Data Guard Broker.
C. The C # # A_ADMIN user can perform wallet operations.
D. The C # # D_ADMIN user can perform backup and recovery operations
   for Automatic Storage Management (ASM).
E. The C # # B_ADMIN user can perform all backup and recovery
   operations using RMAN or SQL* Plus.

Correct Answer: BDE Section: (none) Explanation

Explanation/Reference:

B: SYSDG administrative privilege has ability to perform Data Guard operations (including startup and shutdown) using Data Guard Broker or dgmgrl. D: SYSASM
The new (introduced in 11g) SYSASM role to manage the ASM instance, variable extent sizes to reduce shared pool usage, and the ability of an instance to read from a specific disk of a diskgroup

E (Not A): SYSDBA is like a role in the sense that it is granted, but SYSDBA is a special built-in privilege to allow the DBA full control over the database

Incorrect:
Not C: SYSKM. SYSKM administrative privilege has ability to perform transparent data encryption wallet operations.

Note:
Use the V$PWFILE_USERS view to see the users who have been granted administrative privileges.

QUESTION 83

In your Database, the TBS PERCENT USED parameter is set to 60 and the TBS PERCENT FREE parameter is set to 20.

Which two storage-tiering actions might be automated when using information Lifecycle Management (ILM) to automate data movement? (Choose two.)

A. The movement of all segments to a target tablespace with a higher degree of compression, on a different storage tier, when the source tablespace exceeds TBS PERCENT USED
B. Setting the target tablespace to read-only
C. The movement of some segments to a target tablespace with a higher degree of compression, on a different storage tier, when the source tablespace exceeds TBS PERCENT USED
D. Setting the target tablespace offline
E. The movement of some blocks to a target tablespace with a lower degree of compression, on a different storage tier, when the source tablespace exceeds TBS PERCENT USED

Correct Answer: BC

Explanation/Reference:

The value for TBS_PERCENT_USED specifies the percentage of the tablespace quota when a tablespace is considered full. The value for TBS_PERCENT_FREE specifies the targeted free percentage for the tablespace. When the percentage of the tablespace quota reaches the value of TBS_PERCENT_USED, ADO begins to move data so that percent free of the tablespace quota approaches the value of TBS_PERCENT_FREE. This action by ADO is a best effort and not a guarantee.

QUESTION 84

Which three statements are true about Flashback Database? (Choose three.)

A. Flashback logs are written sequentially, and are archived.
B. Flashback Database uses a restored control file to recover a database.
C. The Oracle database automatically creates, deletes, and resides flashback logs in the Fast Recovery Area.
D. Flashback Database can recover a database to the state that it was in before a reset logs operation.
E. Flashback Database can recover a data file that was dropped during the span of time of the flashback.
F. Flashback logs are used to restore to the blocks before images, and then the redo data may be used to roll forward to the desired flashback time.

Correct Answer: CDF

QUESTION 85

Which statement is true about Enterprise Manager (EM) express in Oracle Database 12c?

A. By default, EM express is available for a database after database creation.
B. You can use EM express to manage multiple databases running on the same server.
C. You can perform basic administrative tasks for pluggable databases by using the EM express interface.

D. You cannot start up or shut down a database Instance by using EM express.
E. You can create and configure pluggable databases by using EM express.

Correct Answer: D

Explanation/Reference:

http://www.oracle.com/technetwork/database/manageability/emx-intro-1965965.html

QUESTION 86

In which two scenarios do you use SQL* Loader to load data? (Choose two.)

A. Transform the data while it is being loaded into the database.
B. Use transparent parallel processing without having to split the external data first.
C. Load data into multiple tables during the same load statement.
D. Generate unique sequential key values in specified columns.

Correct Answer: CD

QUESTION 87

You are connected to a pluggable database (PDB) as a common user with DBA privileges. The STATISTICS_LEVEL parameter is PDB_MODIFIABLE. You execute the following:
SQL > ALTER SYSTEM SET STATISTICS_LEVEL = ALL SID = '*'
SCOPE = SPFILE;

Which is true about the result of this command?

A. The STATISTICS_LEVEL parameter is set to all whenever this PDB is re-opened.
B. The STATISTICS_LEVEL parameter is set to ALL whenever any PDB is reopened.
C. The STATISTICS_LEVEL parameter is set to all whenever the multitenant container database (CDB) is restarted.
D. Nothing happens; because there is no SPFILE for each PDB, the statement is ignored.

Correct Answer: A

QUESTION 88

On your Oracle 12c database, you Issue the following commands to create indexes

SQL > CREATE INDEX oe.ord_customer_ix1 ON oe.orders (customers_id, sales_rep_id) INVISIBLE; SQL> CREATE BITMAP INDEX oe.ord_customer_ix2 ON oe.orders (customers_id, sales_rep_id); Which two statements are correct? (Choose two.)

A. Both the indexes are created; however, only the ORD_COSTOMER index is visible.
B. The optimizer evaluates index access from both the Indexes before deciding on which index to use for query execution plan.
C. Only the ORD_CUSTOMER_IX1 index is created.
D. Only the ORD_CUSTOMER_IX2 index is created.
E. Both the indexes are updated when a new row is inserted, updated, or deleted In the orders table.

Correct Answer: AE

Explanation/Reference:

11G has a new feature called Invisible Indexes. An invisible index is invisible to the optimizer as default. Using this feature we can test a new index without effecting the execution plans of the existing sql statements or we can test the effect of dropping an index without dropping it.

QUESTION 89

Identify three benefits of Unified Auditing.

A. Decreased use of storage to store audit trail rows in the database.
B. It improves overall auditing performance.
C. It guarantees zero-loss auditing.
D. The audit trail cannot be easily modified because it is read-only.
E. It automatically audits Recovery Manager (RMAN) events.

Correct Answer: ABE

Explanation/Reference:

A: Starting with 12c, Oracle has unified all of the auditing types into one single unit called Unified auditing. You don't have to turn on or off all of the different auidting types individually and as a matter of fact auditing is enabled by default right out of the box. The AUD$ and FGA$ tables have been replaced with one single audit trail table. All of the audit data is now stored in Secure Files table thus improving the overall management aspects of audit data itself.
B: Further the audit data can also be buffered solving most of the common performance related problems seen on busy environments.
E: Unified Auditing is able to collect audit data for Fine Grained Audit, RMAN, Data Pump, Label Security, Database Vault and Real Application Security operations.

Note:
* Benefits of the Unified Audit Trail

The benefits of a unified audit trail are many:
/ (B) Overall auditing performance is greatly improved. The default mode that unified audit works is Queued Write mode. In this mode, the audit records are batched in SGA queue and is persisted in a periodic way. Because the audit records are written to SGA queue, there is a significant performance improvement.

/ The unified auditing functionality is always enabled and does not depend on the initialization parameters that were used in previous releases

/ (A) The audit records, including records from the SYS audit trail, for all the audited components of your Oracle Database installation are placed in one location and in one format, rather than your having to look in different places to find audit trails in varying formats. This consolidated view enables auditors to co-relate audit information from different components. For example, if an error occurred during an INSERT statement, standard auditing can indicate the error number and the SQL that was executed. Oracle Database Vault-specific information can indicate whether this error happened because of a command rule violation or realm violation. Note that there will be two audit records with a distinct AUDIT_TYPE. With this unification in place, SYS audit records appear with AUDIT_TYPE set to Standard Audit.

/ The management and security of the audit trail is also improved by having it in single audit trail.

/ You can create named audit policies that enable you to audit the supported components listed at the beginning of this section, as well as SYS administrative users. Furthermore, you can build conditions and exclusions into your policies.

* Oracle Database 12c Unified Auditing enables selective and effective auditing inside the Oracle database using policies and conditions. The new policy based syntax simplifies management of auditing within the database and provides the ability to accelerate auditing based on conditions.

* The new architecture unifies the existing audit trails into a single audit trail, enabling simplified management and increasing the security of audit data generated by the database.

QUESTION 90

You upgraded from a previous Oracle database version to Oracle Database version to Oracle Database 12c. Your database supports a mixed workload. During the day, lots of insert, update, and delete operations are performed. At night, Extract, Transform, Load (ETL) and batch reporting jobs are run. The ETL jobs perform certain database operations using two or more concurrent sessions.

After the upgrade, you notice that the performance of ETL jobs has degraded. To ascertain the cause of performance degradation, you want to collect basic statistics such as the level of parallelism, total database time, and the number of I/O requests for the ETL jobs.

How do you accomplish this?

A. Examine the Active Session History (ASH) reports for the time period of the ETL or batch reporting runs.
B. Enable SQL tracing for the queries in the ETL and batch reporting queries and gather diagnostic data from the trace file.
C. Enable real-time SQL monitoring for ETL jobs and gather diagnostic data from the V$SQL_MONITOR view.
D. Enable real-time database operation monitoring using the DBMS_SQL_MONITOR.BEGIN_OPERATION function, and then use the DBMS_SQL_MONITOR.REPORT_SQL_MONITOR function to view the required information.

Correct Answer: D

Explanation/Reference:

* Monitoring database operations
Real-Time Database Operations Monitoring enables you to monitor long running database tasks such as batch jobs, scheduler jobs, and Extraction, Transformation, and Loading (ETL) jobs as a composite business operation. This feature tracks the progress of SQL and PL/SQL queries associated with the business operation being monitored. As a DBA or developer, you can define business operations for monitoring by explicitly specifying the start and end of the operation or implicitly with tags that identify the operation.

QUESTION 91

Examine the following commands for redefining a table with Virtual Private Database (VPD) policies:

```
BEGIN
   DBMS_RLS.ADD_POLICY (
      object_schema      => 'hr',
      object_name        => 'employees',
      policy_name        => 'employees_policy',
      function_schema    => 'hr',
      policy_function    => 'auth_emp_dep_100',
      statement_types    => 'select, insert, update, delete'
   );
END;

BEGIN
   DBMS_REDEFINITION.START_REDEF_TABLE (
      uname              => 'hr',
      orig_table         => 'employees',
      int_table          => 'int_employees',
      col_mapping        => NULL,
      options_flag       => DBMS_REDEFINITION.CONS_USE_PK,
      orderby_cols       => NULL,
      part_name          => NULL,
      copy_vpd_opt       => DBMS_REDEFINITION.CONS_VPD_AUTO);
END;
```

Which two statements are true about redefining the table? (Choose two.)

A. All the triggers for the table are disabled without changing any of the column names or column types in the table.
B. The primary key constraint on the EMPLOYEES table is disabled during redefinition.

C. VPD policies are copied from the original table to the new table during online redefinition.

D. You must copy the VPD policies manually from the original table to the new table during online redefinition.

Correct Answer: BC

Explanation/Reference:

C (not D): CONS_VPD_AUTO
Used to indicate to copy VPD policies automatically

* DBMS_RLS.ADD_POLICY
/ The DBMS_RLS package contains the fine-grained access control administrative interface, which is used to implement Virtual Private Database (VPD).DBMS_RLS is available with the Enterprise Edition only.

Note:
* CONS_USE_PK and CONS_USE_ROWID are constants used as input to the "options_flag" parameter in both the START_REDEF_TABLE Procedure and CAN_REDEF_TABLE Procedure. CONS_USE_ROWID is used to indicate that the redefinition should be done using rowids while CONS_USE_PK implies that the redefinition should be done using primary keys or pseudo-primary keys (which are unique keys with all component columns having NOT NULL constraints).
* DBMS_REDEFINITION.START_REDEF_TABLE
To achieve online redefinition, incrementally maintainable local materialized views are used. These logs keep track of the changes to the master tables and are used by the materialized views during refresh synchronization.

* START_REDEF_TABLE Procedure
Prior to calling this procedure, you must manually create an empty interim table (in the same schema as the table to be redefined) with the desired attributes of the post-redefinition table, and then call this procedure to initiate the redefinition.

QUESTION 92

Which two statements are true about the use of the procedures listed in the v$sysaux_occupants.move_procedure column? (Choose two.)

A. The procedure may be used for some components to relocate component data to the SYSAUX tablespace from its current tablespace.

B. The procedure may be used for some components to relocate component data from the SYSAUX tablespace to another tablespace.

C. All the components may be moved into SYSAUX tablespace.

D. All the components may be moved from the SYSAUX tablespace.

Correct Answer: AB

QUESTION 93

Which statement is true about Oracle Net Listener?

A. It acts as the listening endpoint for the Oracle database instance for all local and non-local user connections.

B. A single listener can service only one database instance and multiple remote client connections.

C. Service registration with the listener is performed by the process monitor (PMON) process of each database instance.

D. The listener.ora configuration file must be configured with one or more listening protocol addresses to allow remote users to connect to a database instance.

E. The listener.ora configuration file must be located in the ORACLE_HOME/network/admin directly.

Correct Answer: C

Explanation/Reference:

https://docs.oracle.com/database/121/CNCPT/process.htm

QUESTION 94

You are administering a database stored in Automatic Storage Management (ASM). You use RMAN to back up the database and the MD_BACKUP command to back up the ASM metadata regularly. You lost an ASM disk group DG1 due to hardware failure.

In which three ways can you re-create the lost disk group and restore the data? (Choose three.)

A. Use the MD_RESTORE command to restore metadata for an existing disk group by passing the existing disk group name as an input parameter and use RMAN to restore the data.

B. Use the MKDG command to restore the disk group with the same configuration as the backed-up disk group and data on the disk group.

C. Use the MD_RESTORE command to restore the disk group with the changed disk group specification, failure group specification, name, and other attributes and use RMAN to restore the data.

D. Use the MKDG command to restore the disk group with the same configuration as the backed-up disk group name and same set of disks and failure group configuration, and use RMAN to restore the data.

E. Use the MD_RESTORE command to restore both the metadata and data for the failed disk group.

F. Use the MKDG command to add a new disk group DG1 with the same or different specifications for failure group and other attributes and use RMAN to restore the data.

Correct Answer: ACF

Explanation/Reference:

AC (not E):
The md_restore command allows you to restore a disk group from the metadata created by the md_backup command. md_restore can't restore data, only metadata.

QUESTION 95

Which Oracle Database component is audited by default if the unified Auditing option is enabled?

A. Oracle Data Pump
B. Oracle Recovery Manager (RMAN)
C. Oracle Label Security
D. Oracle Database Vault
E. Oracle Real Application Security

Correct Answer: B

QUESTION 96

Your multitenant container (CDB) containing three pluggable databases (PDBs) is running in ARCHIVELOG mode. You find that the SYSAUX tablespace is corrupted in the root container.

The steps to recover the tablespace are as follows:

1. Mount the CDB.
2. Close all the PDBs.
3. Open the database.
4. Apply the archive redo logs.
5. Restore the data file.
6. Take the SYSAUX tablespace offline.

7. Place the SYSAUX tablespace online.
8. Open all the PDBs with RESETLOGS.
9. Open the database with RESETLOGS.
10. Execute the command SHUTDOWN ABORT.
Which option identifies the correct sequence to recover the SYSAUX tablespace? A. 6, 5, 4, 7
B. 10, 1, 2, 5, 8
C. 10, 1, 2, 5, 4, 9, 8
D. 10, 1, 5, 8, 10

Correct Answer: A

Explanation/Reference:

RMAN> ALTER TABLESPACE sysaux OFFLINE IMMEDIATE; RMAN> RESTORE TABLESPACE sysaux;
RMAN> RECOVER TABLESPACE sysaux; RMAN> ALTER TABLESPACE sysaux ONLINE;

* Example:
While evaluating the 12c beta3 I was not able to do the recover while testing "all pdb files lost". Cannot close the pdb as the system datafile was missing...
So only option to recover was:
Shutdown cdb (10)
startup mount; (1)
restore pluggable database recover pluggable database alter database open;
alter pluggable database name open;
Oracle support says: You should be able to close the pdb and restore/recover the system tablespace of PDB.

* Inconsistent backups are usually created by taking online database backups. You can also make an inconsistent backup by backing up data files while a database is closed, either:

/ Immediately after the crash of an Oracle instance (or, in an Oracle RAC configuration, all instances)
/ After shutting down the database using SHUTDOWN ABORT

Inconsistent backups are only useful if the database is in ARCHIVELOG mode and all archived redo logs created since the backup are available.

* Open the database with the RESETLOGS option after finishing recovery:
SQL> ALTER DATABASE OPEN RESETLOGS;

QUESTION 97

Which three are direct benefits of the multiprocess, multithreaded architecture of Oracle Database 12c when it is enabled? (Choose three.)

A. Reduced logical I/O
B. Reduced virtual memory utilization
C. Improved parallel Execution performance
D. Improved Serial Execution performance
E. Reduced physical I/O
F. Reduced CPU utilization

Correct Answer: BCF

Explanation/Reference:

* Multiprocess and Multithreaded Oracle Database Systems

Multiprocess Oracle Database (also called multiuser Oracle Database) uses several processes to run different parts of the Oracle Database code and additional Oracle processes for the users—either one process for each connected user or one or more processes shared by multiple users. Most databases are multiuser because a primary advantage of a database is managing data needed by multiple users simultaneously.

Each process in a database instance performs a specific job. By dividing the work of the database and applications into several processes, multiple users and applications can connect to an instance simultaneously while the system gives good performance.

* In previous releases, Oracle processes did not run as threads on UNIX and Linux systems. Starting in Oracle Database 12c, the multithreaded Oracle Database model enables Oracle processes to execute as operating system threads in separate address spaces.

QUESTION 98

In order to exploit some new storage tiers that have been provisioned by a storage administrator, the partitions of a large heap table must be moved to other tablespaces in your Oracle 12c database?

Both local and global partitioned B-tree Indexes are defined on the table.

A high volume of transactions access the table during the day and a medium volume of transactions access it at night and during weekends.

Minimal disrupt ion to availability is required.

Which three statements are true about this requirement? (Choose three.)

A. The partitions can be moved online to new tablespaces.
B. Global indexes must be rebuilt manually after moving the partitions.
C. The partitions can be compressed in the same tablespaces.
D. The partitions can be compressed in the new tablespaces.
E. Local indexes must be rebuilt manually after moving the partitions.

Correct Answer: ACD

Explanation/Reference:

A: You can create and rebuild indexes online. Therefore, you can update base tables at the same time you are building or rebuilding indexes on that table. You can perform DML operations while the index build is taking place, but DDL operations are not allowed. Parallel execution is not supported when creating or rebuilding an index online.

D: Moving (Rebuilding) Index-Organized Tables
Because index-organized tables are primarily stored in a B-tree index, you can encounter fragmentation as a consequence of incremental updates. However, you can use the ALTER TABLE...MOVE statement to rebuild the index and reduce this fragmentation.

C: If a table can be compressed in the new tablespace, also it can be compressed in the same tablespace.

Incorrect:
Not B, not E: Local and Global indexes can be automatically rebuild with UPDATE INDEXES when you move the table.

QUESTION 99

In your production database, data manipulation language (DML) operations are executed on the SALES table.
You have noticed some dubious values in the SALES table during the last few days. You are able to track users, actions taken, and the time of the action for this particular period but the changes in data are not tracked.
You decide to keep track of both the old data and new data in the table long with the user information. What action would you take to achieve this task?

A. Apply fine-grained auditing.
B. Implement value-based auditing.
C. Impose standard database auditing to audit object privileges.
D. Impose standard database auditing to audit SQL statements.

Correct Answer: B

QUESTION 100

The user SCOTT owns the CUST table that is placed in the SALES tablespace. The user SCOTT opens a session and executes commands as follows:

SQL> INSERT INTO cust VALUES(101, 'JACK');
1 row created.
SQL> INSERT INTO cust VALUES(102, 'SMITH');
1 row created.

As a DBA, you execute the following command from another session:
ALTER TABLESPACE sales READ ONLY;

Which statement is true regarding the effect of this command on the transaction in Scott's session?

A. The command fails as a transaction is still pending.
B. The transaction in Scott's session is rolled back and the tablespace becomes readonly.
C. The command waits and the user SCOTT can execute data manipulation language (DML) statements only as part of the current transaction.

D. The command hangs until all transactions on the objects in the tablespace commit or rollback, and then the tablespace is placed in readonly mode.

Correct Answer: B

QUESTION 101

You plan to implement the distributed database system in your company. You invoke Database Configuration Assistant (DBCA) to create a database on the server. During the installation, DBCA prompts you to specify the Global Database Name.

What must this name be made up of?

A. It must be made up of a database name and a domain name.
B. It must be made up of the value in ORACLE_SID and HOSTNAME.
C. It must be made up of the value that you plan to assign for INSTANCE_NAME and HOSTNAME.
D. It must be made up of the value that you plan to assign for ORACLE_SID and SERVICE_NAMES.

Correct Answer: A

Explanation/Reference:

Using the DBCA to Create a Database (continued)

3. Database Identification: Enter the Global Database Name in The form database_name.domain_name, and the system identifier (SID). The SID defaults lo the database name and uniquely identifies the instance associated with the database.

4. Management Options: Use this page to set up your database so that it can be managed with Oracle Enterprise Manager. Select the default: "Configure the Database with Enterprise Manager." Optionally, this page allows you to configure alert notifications and daily disk backup area settings.

Note:
Yon must configure the listener before you can configure Enterprise Manager (as shown earlier).

QUESTION 102

Which two statements are true about standard database auditing? (Choose two.)

A. DDL statements can be audited.
B. Statements that refer to standalone procedure can be audited.
C. Operations by the users logged on as SYSDBA cannot be audited.
D. Only one audit record is ever created for a session per audited statement even though it is executed more than once.

Correct Answer: AB

QUESTION 103

You executed the following command to create a password file in the database server:
$ orapwd file = orapworcl entries = 5 ignorecase=N

Which statement describes the purpose of the above password file?

A. It records usernames and passwords of users when granted the DBA role
B. It contains usernames and passwords of users for whom auditing is enabled
C. It is used by Oracle to authenticate users for remote database administrator
D. It records usernames and passwords of all users when they are added to OSDBA or OSOPER operating groups

Correct Answer: A

QUESTION 104

Which three statements are true about Oracle Data Pump? (Choose three.)

A. IMPDP can be used to change target data file names, schemas, and tablespaces during import.
B. The DBMS_DATAPUMP PL/SQL package can be used independently of Data Pump clients to perform export and import operations.
C. EXPDP and IMPDP are the client components of Oracle Data Pump.

D. Oracle Data Pump export and import operations can be performed only by users with the `SYSDBA` privilege.

E. `IMPDP` always use the conventional path insert method to import data.

Correct Answer: ABC

Explanation/Reference:

https://docs.oracle.com/cd/E11882_01/server.112/e22490/dp_overview.htm#SUTIL2880

QUESTION 105

Your database instance has started using an SPFILE. Examine the RMAN configuration settings:

```
CONFIGURE RETENTION POLICY TO REDUNDANCY 1; # default
CONFIGURE BACKUP OPTIMIZATION OFF; # default
CONFIGURE DEFAULT DEVICE TYPE TO DISK; # default
CONFIGURE CONTROLFILE AUTOBACKUP ON;
CONFIGURE CONTROLFILE AUTOBACKUP FORMAT FOR DEVICE TYPE DISK TO '%F'; default
```

You execute the command:

```
RMAN> BACKUP AS COPY TABLESPACE TEST;
```

Which three types of files are backed up by using this command? (Choose three.)

A. online redo log files
B. control file
C. SPFILE
D. archived redo log files
E. data file(s)
F. PFILE

Correct Answer: BCE

Explanation/Reference:

http://www.juliandyke.com/Research/RMAN/BackupCommand.php

QUESTION 106

Which three statements are true about Oracle Restart? (Choose three.)

A. It can be configured to automatically attempt to restart various components after a hardware or software failure.
B. While starting any components, it automatically attempts to start all dependencies first and in proper order.
C. It can be configured to automatically restart a database in case of normal shutdown of the database instance.
D. It can be used to only start Oracle components.
E. It runs periodic check operations to monitor the health of Oracle components.

Correct Answer: BDE

QUESTION 107

You want to schedule a job to rebuild a table's indexes after a bulk insert, which must be scheduled as soon as a file containing data arrives on the system.

What would you do to accomplish this?

A. Create a file watcher and an event-based job for bulk insert and then create another job to rebuild indexes on the table.
B. Create a file watcher for the bulk inserts and then create a job to rebuild indexes.
C. Create a job array and add a job for bulk insert and a job to rebuild indexes to the job array.
D. Create an event-based job for the file arrival event, then create a job for bulk insert, and then create a job to rebuild indexes.

Correct Answer: A

QUESTION 108

You execute this command:

```
SQL> CREATE TABLESPACE lmtbsb DATAFILE '/u02/oracle/data/lmtbsb01.dbf' SIZE 50M
     EXTENT MANAGEMENT LOCAL;
```

Which two statements are true about segment space management for segments in this tablespace? (Choose two.)

A. Space utilization inside segments is mapped by bitmaps.
B. Segments are automatically shrunk and compressed when rows are deleted.
C. The `PCTFREE` storage parameter has no effect on segments created in this tablespace.
D. The `PCTUSED` storage parameter has no effect on segments created in this tablespace.

Correct Answer: AD

QUESTION 109

You have successfully taken a database backup by using the command:
```
RMAN> BACKUP AS BACKUPSET DATABASE;
```

Now you execute this command:

```
RMAN> BACKUP INCREMENTAL LEVEL 1 DATABASE;
```

What is the outcome?

A. It fails because an incremental level 1 backup always searches for an image copy as level 0 backup.
B. It fails because an incremental level 0 backup does not exist.
C. It takes a backup of blocks that have been formatted since the last full database backup.
D. It takes an incremental level 0 backup of the database.
E. It first takes an incremental level 0 backup and then an incremental level 1 backup.

Correct Answer: E

Explanation/Reference:

https://docs.oracle.com/cd/B19306_01/backup.102/b14192/bkup004.htm (4.4.1.2)

QUESTION 110

Which two actions does an incremental checkpoint perform? (Choose two.)

A. It signals CKPT to write the checkpoint position to the data file headers.
B. It writes the checkpoint position to the data file headers.
C. It advances the checkpoint position in the checkpoint queue.
D. It writes the checkpoint position to the control file.

Correct Answer: CD

Explanation/Reference:
http://www.dba-oracle.com/t_incremental_checkpoint.htm

QUESTION 111

You want to prevent a group of users in your database from performing long-running transactions that consume huge amounts of space in the undo tablespace. If the quota for these users is exceeded during execution of a data manipulation language (DML) statement, the operation should abort and return an error. However, queries should still be allowed, even if users have exceeded the undo space limitation.

How would you achieve this?

A. Specify the maximum amount of quota a user can be allocated in the undo tablespace.
B. Decrease the number of Interested Transaction List (ITL) slots for the segments on which these users perform transactions.
C. Implement a profile for these users.
D. Implement a Database Resource Manager plan.

Correct Answer: D

QUESTION 112

A database instance is started by using an SPFILE. The database is configured in ARCHIVELOG mode and the control file autobackup is configured. Daily full database backups are performed by using RMAN.

You lost all control files due to media failure.

Given the steps to recover from the error in random order:

1. Shut down the instance, if it is not already down.
2. Restore the control file from autobackup to a new location.
3. Start the database instance to NOMOUNT state.
4. Recover the database to the point of failure of the control file.
5. Open the database with the RESETLOGS option.
6. Mount the database.
7. Update the SPFILE with the new location of the control file by using the ALTER SYSTEM command. Identify the correct sequence of the required steps.

A. 1, 3, 2, 6, 7, 4, 5
B. 1, 3, 7, 2, 6, 4, 5

C. 1, 3, 2, 4, 5
D. 1, 2, 6, 4, 5
E. 1, 6, 2, 4, 5

Correct Answer: A

QUESTION 113

You have just completed a manual upgrade of an Oracle 11g Database to Oracle Database 12c.

The Post-Upgrade Status Tool reports an INVALID status for some of the components after the upgrade. What must you do first in this situation to attempt to fix this problem?

A. Run catuppst.sql to perform revalidation actions
B. Run utluiobj.sql to filter out objects that were invalidated by the upgrade process.
C. Run preupgrd.sql and then execute the generated "fix-up" scripts to resolve status issues.
D. Run utlrp.sql to recompile stored PL/SQL and Java code and check the DBA_REGISTRY view.

Correct Answer: D

QUESTION 114

Examine the parameters for a database instance:

NAME	TYPE	VALUE
temp_undo_enabled	boolean	TRUE
undo_management	string	AUTO
undo_retention	integer	900
undo_tablespace	string	UNDOTBS1

Your database has three undo tablespaces and the default undo tablespace is not autoextensible. Resumable space allocation is not enabled for any sessions in the database instance.

What is the effect on new transactions when all undo space in the default undo tablespace is in use by active transactions?

A. Transactions write their undo in the SYSTEM undo segment.
B. Transactions fail.
C. Transactions wait until space becomes available in UNDOTBS1.
D. Transactions write their undo in a temporary tablespace.

Correct Answer: B

Explanation/Reference:

https://docs.oracle.com/cd/B19306_01/server.102/b14231/undo.htm (undo retention)

QUESTION 115

The DEFERRED_SEGMENT_CREATION parameter is set to TRUE in your database instance. You execute the following command to create a table:

```
SQL> CREATE TABLE acct1
       (ac_no NUMBER,
        ac_desc varchar2(25),
        amount number(10,2));
```

Which two statements are true? (Choose two.)

A. The table is created without a segment because the storage clause is missing.
B. A segment is allocated when the first row is inserted in the table.
C. A segment is allocated when an index is created for any column in the table.
D. The table is created and extents are immediately allocated as per the default storage defined for its tablespace.
E. A segment is allocated for the table if the ALTER TABLE... ALLOCATE EXTENT command is issued.

Correct Answer: BE

QUESTION 116

Which three statements are true about automated maintenance tasks? (Choose three.)

A. They run at predefined time intervals that are intended to occur during a period of low system load.
B. An Oracle Scheduler job is created for each maintenance task that is scheduled to run in a maintenance window.
C. A maintenance window is automatically extended until all the maintenance tasks defined are completed.
D. A repository is maintained in the SYSTEM tablespace to store the history of execution of all tasks.
E. Predefined maintenance tasks consist of automatic optimizer statistics collection, running Automatic Segment Advisor, and running Automatic SQL Tuning Advisor.

Correct Answer: ABE

Explanation/Reference:

https://docs.oracle.com/cd/E11882_01/server.112/e25494/tasks.htm#ADMI N12331

QUESTION 117

Which three statements are true about the purpose of checkpoints?
(Choose three.)

A. They ensure that uncommitted transactions are rolled back in case of an instance failure.
B. They ensure that all the dirty buffers are written to disk during a normal shutdown.
C. They ensure that instance recovery starts in the event of an instance failure.
D. They ensure that dirty buffers in the buffer cache are written to disk regularly.
E. They reduce the time required for recovery in case of an instance failure.

Correct Answer: BDE

Explanation/Reference:

http://docs.oracle.com/cd/E36909_01/server.1111/e25789/startup.htm#BABGDACG

QUESTION 118

The HR user executes the following query on the EMPLOYEES table but does not issue COMMIT, ROLLBACK, or any data definition language (DDL) command
after that:

```
SQL> SELECT job
     FROM employees
     WHERE job='CLERK' FOR UPDATE OF empno;
```

HR then opens a second session.

Which two operations wait when executed in HR's second session?
(Choose two.)

A. LOCK TABLE employees IN EXCLUSIVE MODE;
B. INSERT INTO employees(empno,ename) VALUES (1289, 'Dick');

C. `SELECT job FROM employees WHERE job='CLERK' FOR UPDATE OF empno;`
D. `SELECT empno,ename FROM employees WHERE job='CLERK';`
E. `INSERT INTO employees(empno,ename,job) VALUES (2001,'Harry','CLERK);`

Correct Answer: AC

QUESTION 119

In your database, USERS is the default permanent tablespace. Examine the commands and their outcome:

```
SQL> CREATE USER user02 identified by us123 QUOTA 10M ON users;
User created.

SQL> GRANT create session, sysdba TO user02;
Grant succeeded.
```

You plan to execute the commands:

```
SQL> CONN user02/us123 AS SYSDBA
SQL> CREATE TABLE mytab (id number, lname varchar2(20));
```

Which two statements are true? (Choose two.)

A. The MYTAB table is created in the SYSTEM tablespace but no rows can be inserted into the table by USER02.
B. The MYTAB table is created in the SYSTEM tablespace and rows can be inserted into the table by USER02.
C. The MYTAB table is created in the USERS tablespace but no rows can be inserted into the table by USER02.
D. The CREATE TABLE statement generates an error because the SYSDBA privilege does not provide any space quota on the SYSTEM tablespace by default.
E. The MYTAB table is owned by the SYS user.

Correct Answer: BE

QUESTION 120

You use multiple temporary tables frequently in your database. Which two are benefits of configuring temporary undo? (Choose two.)

A. Performance improves because less redo is written to the redo log.
B. Temporary undo reduces the amount of undo stored in undo tablespaces.
C. Performance improves because data manipulation language (DML) operations performed on temporary tables do not use the buffer cache.
D. Performance improves because no redo and undo are generated for the temporary tables.

Correct Answer: AB

QUESTION 121

Which three statements are true about the Pre-Upgrade Information Tool? (Choose three.)

A. It generates a script to recompile invalid objects post-upgrade.
B. The `preupgrade_fixups.sql` script is created to list and describe issues in the source database.
C. A log file, `preupgrade.log`, is created that contains the output of the Pre-Upgrade Information tool.
D. It checks for required tablespaces and if they are not available, creates them automatically.
E. The `preupgrade_fixups.sql` script is executed automatically to fix issues in the source database.
F. The `postupgrade_fixups.sql` script is created to address issues that can be fixed after a database has been upgraded.

Correct Answer: ACE

Explanation/Reference:

https://docs.oracle.com/database/122/UPGRD/using-preupgrade-information-tool-for-oracle-database.htm#UPGRD-GUID-C0219AF1-AD43-4097- B358-E53E48958647

QUESTION 122

Which activity is audited by default and recorded in the operating system audit trail irrespective of whether or not database auditing is enabled?

A. execution of SQL statements by users connected with the `SYSDBA` privilege
B. creation of a fine-grained audit policy
C. configuration of unified auditing mode
D. usage of the `AUDIT` statement

Correct Answer: A

Explanation/Reference:

https://docs.oracle.com/cd/B28359_01/network.111/b28531/auditing.htm#DBSEG0622

QUESTION 123

You want to create a role that:
- is protected from unauthorized usage
- does not use a password embedded in the application source code or stored in a table
- is enabled for a user based on security policies defined in a PL/SQL package How would you create this role?

A. as a secure application role
B. with definer's rights
C. with global authentication
D. with external authentication

Correct Answer: A

Explanation/Reference:

https://docs.oracle.com/cd/B28359_01/network.111/b28531/authorization.htm#DBSEG97973

QUESTION 124

Your database instance is started by using a server parameter file (SPFILE). You execute the following command to change the value of the `LOG_BUFFER`
initialization parameter:

```
ALTER SYSTEM SET LOG_BUFFER=32 M;
```

What is the outcome of this command?

A. The parameter value is changed and it comes into effect as soon as space becomes available in the SGA.
B. It returns an error because the value of this parameter cannot be changed dynamically.
C. The parameter value is changed and it comes into effect at the next instance startup.
D. It returns an error because `SCOPE` should be set to `MEMORY`.

Correct Answer: B

QUESTION 125

You want to create a database and you have the following:

- Oracle Grid Infrastructure is installed and configured.
- Oracle Database Vault is installed in ORACLE_HOME to be used for this database.
- Oracle Enterprise Manager Cloud Control is available and an agent is deployed on the database server.

Examine the requirements:

1. configuring the database instance to support shared server mode
2. using Automatic Storage Management (ASM) for storing database files.
3. configuring a naming method to help a remote user connect to a database instance
4. configuring the Fast Recovery Area
5. configuring Database Vault
6. configuring Enterprise Manager (EM) Database Express
7. registering with EM Cloud Control
8. configuring remote log archive destinations

9. enabling daily incremental backups
10. configuring a nondefault block size for nondefault block size
tablespaces

Which of these requirements can be met while creating a database by
using the Database Configuration Assistant (DBCA)? A. 1, 2, 4, 5, 7, 8, 9
and 10

B. 1, 2, 4, 5, 6 and 7
C. 1, 2, 3, 8, 9 and 10
D. 1, 2, 3, 4, 6, 8, 9 and 10
E. 1, 2, 4, 5, 6, 7 and 8

Correct Answer: D

QUESTION 126

You want execution of large database operations to suspend, and then
resume, in the event of space allocation failures. You set the value of the
initialization parameter RESUMABLE_TIMEOUT to 3600.
Which two statements are true? (Choose two.)

A. Before a statement executes in resumable mode, the ALTER SESSION
   ENABLE RESUMABLE statement must be issued in its session.
B. Data Manipulation Language (DML) operations are resumable,
   provided that they are not embedded in a PL/SQL block.
C. A resumable statement can be suspended and resumed only once
   during execution.
D. A suspended statement will report an error if no corrective action has
   taken place during a timeout period.
E. Suspending a statement automatically results in suspending a
   transaction and releasing all the resources held by the transaction.

Correct Answer: AD

QUESTION 127

Which two statements are true about Automatic Database Diagnostic
Monitor (ADDM)? (Choose two.)

A. It calls SQL advisors automatically if required.
B. It provides recommendations only for poorly performing SQL

statements.

C. Its results are stored in AWR.

D. It runs automatically after each AWR snapshot is created and requires at least two snapshots for analysis.

E. It requires at least one Automatic Workload Repository (AWR) snapshot for analysis.

Correct Answer: CE :

QUESTION 128

Which statement is true about using the Database Upgrade Assistant (DBUA) to upgrade your database from Oracle Database 11g to Oracle Database 12c?

A. It terminates if the SYSTEM tablespace in the source database is not autoextensible.

B. It automatically makes necessary changes to Oracle environment variables.

C. It automatically enables unified auditing in the upgraded database.

D. It automatically adds new data files if there is not enough disk space to grow.

Correct Answer: D

Explanation/Reference:

https://docs.oracle.com/cd/E18283_01/server.112/e17222/upgrade.htm#in sertedID5

QUESTION 129

Identify two prerequisites for configuring Enterprise Manager Database Express (EM Express).

A. Grant the APEX_PUBLIC_USER role to the SYSMAN user.

B. Use the DBMS_XDB_CONFIG.SETHTTPPORT procedure to configure a port number for Oracle HTTP Server.

C. Install Oracle HTTP Server.

D. Configure at least one dispatcher for the TCP/IP protocol.

E. Create a `SYSMAN` user with the `SYSDBA` privilege as an administrator for EM Express.

Correct Answer: DE

QUESTION 130

Your database supports a Decision Support System (DSS) workload that involves the execution of complex queries. Currently, the database is running with peak workload. You want to analyze some of the most resource-intensive statements cached in the library cache.

What must you run to receive recommendations on the efficient use of indexes and materialized views to improve query performance?

A. Automatic Database Diagnostic Monitor (ADDM)
B. SQL Tuning Advisor
C. SQL Access Advisor
D. SQL Performance Analyzer
E. Automatic Workload Repository (AWR) report

Correct Answer: C

Explanation/Reference:

https://docs.oracle.com/cd/B28359_01/server.111/b28314/tdpdw_perform.htm#TDPDW00813

QUESTION 131

In which situations does the Database Writer process (`DBWn`) write to data files? (choose two).

A. when the RMAN recovery process starts
B. when a user process commits a transaction
C. when a tablespace is made read-only or taken offline
D. when PMON cleans up dirty buffers in the database buffer cache
E. when clean buffers for reading new blocks into the database buffer cache are not found easily

Correct Answer: BD

Explanation/Reference:

QUESTION 132

Which two statements are true about availability audit features after migration to unified auditing? (Choose two.)

A. The ability of users to audit their own schema objects is not available in the post-migrated database.
B. Operating system audit trail is available in the post-migrated database.
C. Network auditing is available in the post-migrated database.
D. Mandatory auditing of audit administrative actions is available in the post-migrated database.

Correct Answer: AD

Explanation/Reference:

QUESTION 133

Which three statements are true about Database Resource Manager? (Choose three.)
A. A resource plan change can be automated by using the Oracle Scheduler.
B. It can be used to control the consumption of only physical I/Os where excessive physical I/Os can trigger an automatic session termination but excessive logical I/Os cannot.
C. It can be used to control the usage of the undo tablespace by consumer groups.
D. A resource plan can have multiple resource plan directives, each of which controls resource allocation for a different consumer group.
E. It can be used to enable resumable timeout for user sessions.
F. It can be used to control the usage of the temp tablespace by consumer groups.

Correct Answer: ACD

QUESTION 134

What is the effect of setting the `STATISTICS_LEVEL` initialization parameter to `BASIC`?

A. Optimizer statistics are collected automatically.
B. Only timed operating system (OS) statistics and plan execution statistics are collected.
C. Automatic Workload Repository (AWR) snapshots are not generated automatically.
D. The Oracle server dynamically generates the necessary object-level statistics on tables as part of query optimization.

Correct Answer: C

Explanation/Reference:

https://docs.oracle.com/cd/B28359_01/server.111/b28320/initparams240.htm#REFRN10214

QUESTION 135

You are administering a database that supports an OLTP workload.

The default `UNDO` tablespace is a fixed size tablespace with the `RETENTION NOGUARATNEE` clause and undo retention set to 12 minutes. The user `SCOTT` queries a large table during peak activity.
The query runs for more than 15 minutes and then `SCOTT` receives the following error:

`ORA-01555: snapshot too old`

Which is possible reason for this?

A. The Oracle server is unable to generate a read-consistent image for a block containing updates.committed after the query began.
B. The query is unable to place data blocks in the `UNDO` tablespace.
C. The flashback data archive is not enabled for the table on which the query is issued.
D. There is not enough space in Fast Recovery Area.

E. The Oracle server is unable to generate a read-consistent image for a block containing uncommitted updates.

Correct Answer: A

QUESTION 136

Which two categories of segments are analyzed by the Automatic Segment Advisor? (Choose two.)

A. segments in tablespaces that have exceeded a critical or warning space threshold
B. segments that have the highest growth rate in a database
C. segments that are sparsely populated and have more than 10% of free space below the high water mark.
D. segments that have unusable indexes
E. segments for tables created using ADVANCED ROW COMPRESSION

Correct Answer: AB

Explanation/Reference:

http://www.dba-oracle.com/t_segment_advisor_10g.htm

QUESTION 137

Automatic Shared Memory Management (ASMM) is enabled for your database instance. You execute the following command:

```
SQL> ALTER SYSTEM SET DB_CACHE_SIZE = 100M;
```

Which statement is true?

A. It succeeds and the minimum size for the DEFAULT buffer pool is set to 100M.
B. It fails because DB_CACHE_SIZE is a static initialization parameter.
C. It fails because ASMM is enabled and individual SGA components cannot be sized.
D. It succeeds and the value is changed in the SPFILE immediately, but the change takes effect only at the next instance startup.

Correct Answer: A

QUESTION 138

You want to create a database with a block size other than the default 8 kilobytes (KB) by using the Database Configuration Assistant (DBCA).

Which option should you use?

A. Automatic Storage Management (ASM) for storage of data files
B. a file system for storage of data files
C. a Data Warehouse database template
D. a custom database template

Correct Answer: D

QUESTION 139

Which two statements are true about using SQL*Loader? (Choose two.)

A. It can load data from external files by using the direct path only.
B. It can load data into multiple tables using the same load statement.
C. It can load data into only one table at a time.
D. It can generate unique sequential key values in specified columns.
E. It can load data from external files by using the conventional path only.

Correct Answer: AC

QUESTION 140

The HR user owns the BONUSES table. HR grants privileges to the user TOM by using the command:

```
SQL> GRANT SELECT ON bonuses TO tom WITH GRANT OPTION;
```

TOM then executes this command to grant privileges to the user JIM:

```
SQL> GRANT SELET ON hr.bonuses TO jim;
```

Which statement is true?

A. TOM cannot revoke the SELECT ON HR.BONUSES privilege from JIM.
B. HR can revoke the SELECT ON HR.BONUSES privilege from JIM.
C. JIM can grant the SELECT ON HR.BONUSES privilege to other users, but cannot revoke the privilege from them.
D. HR can revoke the SELECT ON HR.BONUSES privilege from TOM, which will automatically revoke the SELECT ON HR.BONUSES privilege from JIM.

Correct Answer: D

QUESTION 141

Your database is running in NOARCHIVLOG mode. Examine the following parameters:

```
Name                      Type      Value
--------------------      --------  ------------------
log_archive_dest          string
log_archive_dest_1        string
db_recovery_file_dest     string    /u01/app/oracle/fast_recovery_area
```

You execute the following command after performing a STARTUP MOUNT:
SQL> ALTER DATABASE ARCHIVELOG;

Which statement is true about the execution of the command?

A. It executes successfully and sets the Fast Recovery Area as the local archive destination.
B. It executes successfully and issues a warning to set LOG_ARCHIVE_DEST while opening the database.
C. It fails and returns an error about LOG_ARCHIVE_DEST not being set.
D. It executes successfully and sets $ORACLE_HOME/dbs as the default archive destination.

Correct Answer: A

QUESTION 142

What is the benefit of running the `catctl.pl` script during an upgrade of a pre-12c database to an Oracle 12c database?

A. It provides a summary of the upgrade results.
B. It recompiles all invalid PL/SQL and Java code.
C. It generates a log file containing the fixes that can be made to the source database.
D. It provides parallel upgrade options to finish the upgrade process with a reduced down time.
E. It generates fix-up scripts to be run on the source database before upgrade.

Correct Answer: D

Explanation/Reference:

https://docs.oracle.com/database/121/UPGRD/upgrade.htm#UPGRD5286 0

QUESTION 143

Which statement is true about redo log files during instance recovery?

A. All current, online, and archived redo logs are required to complete instance recovery.
B. All redo log entries in the current and active logs are applied to data files to reconstruct changes made after the most recent checkpoint.
C. All redo log entries in the current log are applied to data files until the checkpoint position is reached.
D. All current, active, and inactive redo logs are required to complete instance recovery.

Correct Answer: C

Explanation/Reference:

https://docs.oracle.com/cd/A58617_01/server.804/a58396/ch2.htm

QUESTION 144

Your database is running in `ARCHIVELOG` mode. You want to take a consistent whole database backup. Which two statements are true in this scenario? (Choose two.)

A. The user-managed backup consists of only formatted data blocks.
B. The database must be shut down to take a user-managed backup.
C. The RMAN backup contains only data files.
D. The RMAN backup can be performed while the database is open.
E. The database must be in `MOUNT` state to take RMAN backup.

Correct Answer: AB

QUESTION 145

Your database is configured for `ARCHIVELOG` mode, and a daily full database backup is taken. RMAN is configured to perform control file autobackup. In which three scenarios do you need media recovery? (Choose three.)

A. loss of all the copies of the control file
B. loss of all the inactive online redo log group members
C. loss of a data file that belongs to the active undo tablespace
D. loss of data files that belong to the `SYSTEM` tablespace
E. logical corruption of data that is caused by a wrong transaction
F. abnormal termination of the database instance

Correct Answer: ACD

QUESTION 146

Which two statements are true about Oracle Data Pump export and import operations? (Choose two.)

A. You cannot specify how partitioned tables should be handled during an import operation.
B. Only data can be compressed during an export operation.
C. Existing dump files can be overwritten during an export operation.

D. Tables cannot be renamed during an import operation.
E. Metadata that is exported and imported can be filtered based on objects and object types.

Correct Answer: AE

Explanation/Reference:

https://docs.oracle.com/cd/B28359_01/server.111/b28300/expimp.htm#UPGRD12560

QUESTION 147

Your database instance has the following parameter setting:

OS_AUTHENT_PREFIX = OPS$

You execute the following command:

```
SQL> CREATE USER ops$guest_user
         IDENTIFIED EXTERNALLY
         DEFAULT TABLESPACE users;
```

And then grant OPS$GUEST_USER the CREATE SESSION privilege. Which two statements are true? (Choose two.)

A. GUEST_USER can query the tables created in the USERS tablespace by default.
B. The authentication details for GUEST_USER are stored in the database password file.
C. A local GUEST_USER OS account should exist before GUEST_USER can log on to the database.
D. GUEST_USER can log on to the database without specifying a username and password.
E. GUEST_USER is forced to change the password at the first login.

Correct Answer: CD

QUESTION 148

Your database has been running with a peak load for the past hour. You want to preserve the performance statistics collected during this period for comparison when you analyze the performance of the database later.

What must you do to achieve this?

A. Increase the window size of the moving window baseline so that it equals the Automatic Workload Repository (AWR) snapshot retention period.
B. Create a baseline on a pair of snapshots that span the peak load period.
C. Generate Active Session History reports for the peak load period.
D. Set the snapshot retention period in AWR to 60 to avoid automatic purging of snapshots for the past hour.

Correct Answer: B

QUESTION 149

Which four operations performed after the Oracle Restart installation are automatically added to the Oracle Restart configuration? (Choose four.)

A. listener configured by using NETCA
B. database service created by using SRVCTL
C. database created by using a SQL statement
D. database created by using DBCA
E. ASM instance created by using ASMCA
F. database service created by using DBMS_SERVICE.CREATE_SERVICE
G. database service created by modifying the SERVICE_NAMES initialization parameter

Correct Answer: BCEF

Explanation/Reference:

https://docs.oracle.com/cd/E18283_01/server.112/e17120/restart002.htm#insertedID3

QUESTION 150

Your single-instance Oracle 12c database home currently supports conventional auditing and uses Automatic Storage Management (ASM). You want to enable unified auditing by executing the command:

```
$ make -fins_rdbms.mk uniaud_on ioracle
ORACLE_HOME=$ORACLE_HOME
```

Which two steps should you perform before executing this command? (Choose two.)

A. Ensure that the initialization parameter AUDIT_TRAIL is set to DB.
B. Drop any existing fine-grained audit (FGA) policies.
C. Stop the listener.
D. Shut down the database instance.
E. Disable auditing by setting the initialization parameter AUDIT_TRAIL to NONE.

Correct Answer: CE

Explanation/Reference:

https://blogs.oracle.com/UPGRADE/entry/unified_auditing_is_it_on

QUESTION 151

You create an Oracle 12c database and then import schemas that are required by an application which has not yet been developed. You want to get advice on creation of or modifications to indexes, materialized views and partitioning in these schemas.
What must you run to achieve this?

A. SQL Access Advisor with a SQL tuning set
B. Automatic Database Diagnostic Monitor (ADDM) report
C. SQL Tuning Advisor
D. SQL Access Advisor with a hypothetical workload
E. SQL Performance Analyzer

Correct Answer: D

QUESTION 152

The HR user updates the salary of one of the employees in the non-partitioned EMPLOYEES table, but does not commit the transaction. Which two types of lock exist in this situation? (Choose two.)

A. exclusive lock on the EMPLOYEES table
B. null lock on the row being updated
C. null lock on the EMPLOYEES table
D. row level lock on the row being updated
E. shared lock on the EMPLOYEES table

Correct Answer: DE

QUESTION 153

For which three requirements would you use the Database Resource Manager? (Choose three.)

A. specifying an idle time limit that applies to sessions that are idle and blocking other sessions
B. limiting the degree of parallelism of operations performed by user sessions in a consumer group
C. specifying the maximum number of concurrent sessions allowed for a user
D. limiting the CPU used per database call
E. specifying the amount of private space a session can allocate in the shared pool of the SGA.

Correct Answer: ABC

Explanation/Reference:

http://docs.oracle.com/cd/B19306_01/server.102/b14231/dbrm.htm

QUESTION 154

In your database instance, the UNDO_RETENTION parameter is set to 1000 and undo retention is not guaranteed for the fixed size undo tablespace. Which statement is true about undo retention?

A. Undo is retained in the UNDO tablespace for 1000 seconds, and then moved to the SYSTEM tablespace to provide read consistency.
B. Inactive undo is retained for at least 1000 seconds if free undo space is available.
C. Inactive undo is retained for 1000 seconds even if new transactions fall due to lack of space in the undo tablespace.
D. Undo becomes expired obsolete after 1000 seconds.

Correct Answer: B

QUESTION 155

Which two files must you copy from the Oracle home of the database that is being upgraded to the new Oracle home for Oracle Database 12c? (Choose three.)

A. the `tnsnames.ora` file
B. the `sqlnet.ora` file
C. the initialization parameter file
D. the password file
E. the `listener.ora` file

Correct Answer: ABE

Explanation/Reference:

https://docs.oracle.com/cd/E11882_01/server.112/e23633/afterup.htm#UPGRD52747

QUESTION 156

In your Oracle 12c database, you invoke SQL *Loader Express Mode command to load data:

```
$> sqlldr hr/hr table=employees
```

Which two statements are true about this command? (Choose two.)

A. It succeeds and creates the `EMPLOYEES` table in the `HR` schema if the table does not exist.
B. It fails because the SQL *Loader control file location is not specified.
C. It fails because the SQL *Loader data file location is not specified.

D. It succeeds with default settings if the `EMPLOYEES` table belonging to the `HR` schema is already defined in the database.
E. It succeeds even if the `HR` user does not have the `CREATE DIRECTORY` privilege.

Correct Answer: DE

QUESTION 157

Backup requirements for a database:

* Level 0 backup on Sunday
* Cumulative incremental level 1 backup on Monday, Wednesday, and Saturday
* Differential incremental level 1 backup on Tuesday, Thursday, and Friday
Which three statements are true about the strategy? (Choose three.)

A. Level 0 backup on Sunday contains all the blocks that have been formatted.
B. Level 0 backup on Sunday contains all the blocks that have been changed since the last level 1 backup.
C. Level 1 backup on Tuesday, Thursday, and Friday contains all the blocks that have been changed since the last level 1 backup.
D. Level 1 backup on Monday, Wednesday, and Saturday contains all the blocks that have been changed since the last level 0 backup.
E. Level 1 backup on Tuesday, Thursday, and Friday contains all the blocks that have been changed since the last level 0 backup.

Correct Answer: BDE

QUESTION 158

Which two statements are true about the Database Configuration Assistant (DBCA)? (Choose two.)

A. It can be used to create a database template from an existing database.
B. It can be used to add a new tablespace.
C. It can generate SQL database creation scripts.
D. It can be used to copy an existing Oracle database to a new host and apply any patches necessary in the new host.

E. It can configure Automatic Storage Management (ASM) diskgroups.

Correct Answer: AC

Explanation/Reference:
https://docs.oracle.com/cd/E17559_01/em.111/e16599/appdx_creating_db
_templates.htm#CJACEDCD

QUESTION 159

You are managing an Oracle Database 12c database. The database is
open, and you plan to perform Recovery Manager (RMAN) backups. Which
three statements are true about these backups? (Choose three.)
A. The backups would be consistent.
B. The backups would be possible only if the database is running in
   ARCHIVELOG mode.
C. The backups need to be restored and the database has to be
   recovered in case of a media failure.
D. The backups would be inconsistent.
E. The backups by default consist of all the data blocks within the chosen
   files or the full database.

Correct Answer: BCD

Explanation/Reference:

https://docs.oracle.com/cd/E18283_01/server.112/e10897/backrest.htm#in
sertedID4

QUESTION 160

Which three tools or tasks are run by default as part automated
maintenance tasks? (Choose three.)

A. Automatic Database Diagnostic Monitor

B. optimizer statistics gathering

C. SQL Access Advisor

D. Segment Advisor

E. Automatic SQL Tuning Advisor

Correct Answer: BDE Section: (none) Explanation

QUESTION 161

You plan to upgrade your Oracle Database 9i to Oracle Database 12c.
Which two methods can you use? (Choose two.)

A. Perform a rolling upgrade.
B. Perform a direct upgrade by running the Database Upgrade Assistant
   (DBUA).
C. Perform a direct upgrade by manually running the `catctl.pl` and
   `catupgrd.sql` scripts before issuing the `STARTUPUPGRADE`
   command.
D. Install the Oracle Database 12c software, create a new Oracle 12c
   database, and then use the Oracle Data Pump to import data from the
   source Oracle 9i database to the target Oracle 12c database.
E. Upgrade your current database to Oracle Database release 10.2.0.5,
   and then upgrade to Oracle Database 12c.

Correct Answer: CD

QUESTION 162

Examine the following command:

```
SQL> DBMS_STATS. SET_TABLE_PREFS ('SH', 'CUSTOMERS',
'PUBLISH', 'false');
```

What is the effect of executing this command?

A. Existing statistics for the CUSTOMERS table become unusable for the
   query optimizer.
B. Automatic statistics collection is stopped for the CUSTOMERS table.
C. Statistics for the CUSTOMERS table are locked and cannot be
   overwritten.
D. Statistics subsequently gathered on the CUSTOMERS table are stored as
   pending statistics.

Correct Answer: D

QUESTION 163

You install Oracle Grid Infrastructure for a standalone server.

Which two components are automatically included in the Oracle Restart configuration? (Choose two.)

A. A pre-existing Oracle Net Listener
B. Oracle Notification services
C. A pre-existing database
D. A pre-existing Oracle management agent
E. Oracle CSSD service

Correct Answer: BE

Explanation/Reference:

https://docs.oracle.com/database/121/LADBI/oraclerestart.htm#LADBI999

QUESTION 164

In your database, the STATISTICS_LEVEL parameter is set to TYPICAL and an Automatic Workload Repository (AWR) snapshot is taken every 30 minutes.

Which two statements are true about the Automatic Database Diagnostic Monitor (ADDM)? (Choose two.)

A. It measures database performance by analyzing the wait time and CPU time of all non-idle user sessions.
B. It always compares the latest snapshot with the baseline snapshot for analysis.
C. It runs after each AWR snapshot is created and it requires at least two snapshots for analysis.
D. It requires at least four AWR snapshots for analysis.
E. It calls other advisors if required, but does not provide recommendations about the advisors to be used.

Correct Answer: AC

QUESTION 165

Your database is configured in ARCHIVELOG mode, and a daily full
database backup is taken by using RMAN. Control file autobackup is
configured. Loss of which three database files can lead to an incomplete
recovery? (Choose three.)

A. inactive online redo log file group
B. a data file belonging to the default temporary tablespace
C. a data file belonging to the SYSAUX tablespace
D. server parameter file (SPFILE)
E. active online redo log file group
F. all the control flies

Correct Answer: AEF

QUESTION 166

Which two statements are true about resumable space allocation? (Choose
two.)

A. A database-level LOGON trigger can be used to automatically configure
   resumable statement settings for individual sessions.
B. SELECT statements that run out of temporary space for sort areas are
   candidates for resumable execution.
C. A resumable statement can be suspended and resumed only once
   during a session.
D. Resumable space allocation does not apply when a database instance
   uses asynchronous commit.
E. Resumable space allocation does not apply when users exceed their
   assigned space quota in a tablespace.
F. Free space in a segment is automatically reclaimed when a resumable
   statement is suspended because of an out-of-space condition.

Correct Answer: AB

QUESTION 167

Your database supports an online transaction processing (OLTP) workload
in which one of the applications creates a temporary table for a session

and performs transactions on it. This consumes a lot of undo tablespace and generates lots of redo.

Which two actions would you take to solve this problem? (Choose two.)

A. Increase the size of the temporary tablespace.
B. Enable Automatic Memory Management (AMM).
C. Enable undo retention guarantee.
D. Enable temporary undo for the database.
E. Increase the size of the redo log buffer.

Correct Answer: AD

QUESTION 168

You want to create a file watcher and an event-based job for detecting the arrival of files on the local server from various locations. To achieve this, you enable the raising of file arrival events from remote systems.

Which two conditions must be satisfied to receive file arrival events from a remote system? (Choose two.)

A. The remote system must have a running Oracle Database instance and a scheduler agent installed.
B. The initialization parameter REMOTE_OS_AUTHENT must be set to TRUE on your database.
C. The local database must be set up to run remote external jobs.
D. The remote system's scheduler agent must be registered with your database.
E. Database links to remote databases must be created.

Correct Answer: AC

Explanation/Reference:

https://docs.oracle.com/cd/E18283_01/server.112/e17120/scheduse005.htm

QUESTION 169

Unified auditing is enabled in your database. The `HR_ADMIN` and `OE_ADMIN` roles exist and are granted system privileges. You execute the command:

```
SQL>CREATE AUDIT POLICY table_aud PRIVILEGES CREATE ANY
TABLE, DROP ANY TABLE ROLES
hr_admin, oe_admin;
```

Which statement is true?

A. It succeeds and needs to be enabled to capture all SQL statements that require either the specified privileges or any privilege granted to the `HR_ADMIN` and `OE_ADMIN` role.
B. It fails because system privileges cannot be granted with roles in the same audit policy.
C. It succeeds and starts capturing only successful SQL statements for all users who have either the specified privileges or roles granted to them.
D. It fails because the command does not specify when the unified audit policy should be enforced.

Correct Answer: C

QUESTION 170

You determine that database performance is sub-optimal due to hard parsing statements. Automatic Shared Memory Management (ASMM) is disabled for your database instance.

Which tool would you use to get advice on how to improve performance?

A. Memory Advisor for the PGA
B. SQL Access Advisor
C. Memory Advisor for the shared pool
D. SQL Tuning Advisor

Correct Answer: C

Explanation/Reference:

http://docs.oracle.com/cd/E25178_01/server.1111/e10897/montune.htm#CHDGFCFJ

QUESTION 171

Identify three uses of the CROSSCHECK command (Choose three.)

A. to validate the database backup
B. to synchronize logical backup records with physical files in backup storage
C. to check the obsolete backups that can be deleted from the file system
D. to update information about backups that are deleted, corrupted, or inaccessible in a recovery catalog or control file
E. to update the recovery catalog or control file if archived log files are deleted with operating system commands

Correct Answer: BDE

QUESTION 172

Which statement is true about the Oracle central inventory directory (oraInventory)?

A. oraInventory must not be shared by all Oracle software installations on a single system.
B. If ORACLE_BASE is set to /u01/app/oracle for the oracle user during an installation, OUI creates the Oracle Inventory directory in the /u01/app/oracle/ oraInventory path.
C. If an OFA-compliant path is not created and the ORACLE_BASE environment variable is not set during an Oracle Database installation, the Oracle Inventory directory is placed in the home directory of the user that is performing the installation.
D. Oracle software owners must be members of the same central oraInventory group, but they need not have this group as their primary group.

Correct Answer: D

Explanation/Reference:

https://docs.oracle.com/database/121/CWLIN/usrgrps.htm#CWLIN483

QUESTION 173

Which three statements are true about Automatic Workload Repository (AWR)? (Choose three.)

A. An AWR snapshot shows the SQL statements that are producing the highest load on the system, based on criteria such as elapsed time and CPU time.
B. AWR data is stored in memory and in a database.
C. All AWR tables belong to the SYSTEM schema.
D. The manageability monitor (MMON) process gathers statistics and creates an AWR snapshot that is used by the self-tuning components in a database.
E. An AWR snapshot contains system-wide tracing and logging information.

Correct Answer: ABD

QUESTION 174

You want to import the schema objects of the HR user from the development database DEVDB to the production database PRODDB by using Oracle Data Pump. A database link devdb.us.oracle.com is created between PRODDB and DEVDB.

You execute the following command on the PRODDB database server:

```
$ impdp system/manager directory = DB_DATA
  dumpfile = schemas.dat
  schemas = hr
  flashback_time = "TO_TIMESTAMP ('05-01-2012 14:35:00', 'DD-MM-
YYYY HH24:MI:SS')"
```

The command fails, displaying the following error:

```
ORA-39001: invalid argument value
ORA-39000: bad dump file specification
ORA-31640: unable to open dump file "/home/oracle/schema/schemas.
dat" for read
ORA-27037: unable to obtain file status
```

What should you do to resolve the error?

A. Add network_link = devdb.us.oracle.com.

B. Add the `SYSTEM` user to the `schemas` option.
C. Change the `dumpfile` option value to `schema.dat@devdb.us.oracle.com`.
D. Replace the `schemas` option with `network_link = devdb.us.oracle.com`.
E. Replace the `dumpfile` option with `network_link = devdb.us.oracle.com`.

Correct Answer: E

QUESTION 175

Which three statements are true about server-generated alerts? (Choose three.)

A. Server-generated alerts notify administrators of problems that cannot be resolved automatically.
B. Alerts are not issued for locally managed read-only tablespaces.
C. Response actions cannot be specified for server-generated alerts.
D. Stateful alerts can be queried only from the `DBA_ALERT_HISTORY` view.
E. When an alert is cleared, it is moved to the `DBA_ALERT_HISTORY` view.

Correct Answer: ABE

Explanation/Reference:

https://docs.oracle.com/cd/B28359_01/server.111/b28310/schema001.htm#ADMIN10120

QUESTION 176

Which two statements are true about Automatic Storage Management (ASM)? (Choose two.)

A. It mounts databases and diskgroups to make ASM files available to database instances.
B. It spreads files proportionally across all disks in a diskgroup, aiming to

ensure that all the disks in a diskgroup have the same I/O load.

C. It automatically places each disk from an external redundancy diskgroup in its own failure group.
D. It divides files into extents and allows an extent to span disks.
E. It mirrors data at the allocation unit (AU) level across failure groups within a normal or high redundancydiskgroup.

Correct Answer: BC

QUESTION 177

You want to create a test database as a replica of your production database with minimum intervention from a DBA. Which method would you use?

A. Use DBCA to create a template from the existing database to contain the database structure and then manually copy the data by using Oracle Data Pump.
B. Use Database Configuration Assistant (DBCA) to create a template from the existing database to contain the database structure.
C. Create the database by using the CREATE DATABASE. . . command and manually import data by using Data Pump.
D. Use DBCA to create a template from the existing database to contain the database structure with data files and then use the same template to create the database in the new location.

Correct Answer: A

QUESTION 178

You want to load data from a large file into your database without causing an overhead on the SGA.

Which tool would you use.

A. external table
B. Oracle data Pump
C. SQL*Loader with a direct data path
D. SQL*Loader with a conventional data path
E. Enterprise Manager Database Express

Correct Answer: C

Explanation/Reference:

QUESTION 179

As part of a manual upgrade of your database to Oracle Database 12c, you plan to issue the command:
```
SQL> STARTUP UPGRADE
```

Which three statements are true about the upgrade process? (Choose three.)

A. All system triggers are disabled during the upgrade process.
B. Only queries on fixed views execute without errors until you run the `catctl.pl` script.
C. The `COMPATIBLE` parameter must be set to at least 12.1.0 before issuing the command.
D. All job queues remain active during the upgrade process.
E. Only connections `AS SYSDBA` are allowed during the upgrade process.

Correct Answer: ADE

QUESTION 180

Which statement is true about using the Export/Import method for migrating data when upgrading to Oracle Database 12c?

A. It automatically restarts a Data Pump Export or Import job after a failure is connected and the job continues from the point of failure.
B. It can be used to migrate a database only if the source and target databases are hosted on the same endian format.
C. It can be used to migrate a database only if the source database does not have any tablespace in read-only mode.
D. It allows migration of a database directly over network links.

Correct Answer: D

QUESTION 181

Your database is in ARCHIVELOG mode and you want to automate the backup scheduling for your database. Which two tools or utilities would you use to achieve this? (Choose two.)

A. Oracle Enterprise Manager Database Express (EM Express)
B. Oracle Enterprise Manager Cloud Control
C. Database Configuration Assistant (DBCA)
D. Recovery Manager (RMAN) script invoked by using scheduler

Correct Answer: BD

QUESTION 182

Which three functions can be performed by the SQL Tuning Advisor? (Choose three.)

A. recommending creation of indexes based on SQL workload
B. recommending restructuring of SQL statements that have suboptimal plans
C. checking schema objects for missing and state statistics
D. recommending optimization of materialized views
E. generating SQL profiles

Correct Answer: BCE

QUESTION 183

Examine the parameters:

Examine the parameters:

```
NAME                              TYPE            VALUE
-------------------------------   --------------  -------------
resource_limit                    boolean         TRUE
resoucce_manager_cpu_allocation   integer         2
resoucce_manager_plan             string          MY_PLAN
```

Users complain that their sessions for certain transactions hang. You investigate and discover that some users fail to complete their transactions, causing other transactions to wait on row-level locks.

Which two actions would you take to prevent this problem? (Choose two.)

A. Increase the maximum number of ITL slots for segments on which a blocking user performs a transaction.
B. Decrease the SESSIONS_PER_USER limit in the profiles assigned to blocking users.
C. Set a limit in the profiles of blocking users to control the number of data blocks that can be accessed in a session.
D. Use Database Resource Manager to automatically kill the sessions that are idle and are blocking other sessions.
E. Decrease the IDLE_TIME resource limit in the profiles assigned to blocking users.

Correct Answer: BD

QUESTION 184

Examine the following steps:

A DBA grants the CREATE TABLE system privilege with ADMIN OPTION to the user SIDNEY. SIDNEY grants the CREATE TABLE system privilege to the HR user.

Which statement is true?

A. SIDNEY can revoke the CREATE TABLE system privilege only from HR, to whom he granted it.
B. HR can grant the CREATE TABLE system privilege to other users.
C. Neither SIDNEY nor HR can create new tables if the DBA revokes the CREATE TABLE privilege from SIDNEY.
D. HR still retains the CREATE TABLE system privilege if the DBA revokes the CREATE TABLE privilege from SIDNEY.

Correct Answer: C

Explanation/Reference:

http://www.dba-oracle.com/t_with_grant_admin_privileges.htm

QUESTION 185

What is pre-requisite to alter a role?

A. You should be granted the DBA role.
B. You should set the OS_ROLES parameter to true.
C. You should be granted the role with the GRANT OPTION.
D. You should have the ALTER ANY ROLE system privilege.

Correct Answer: D

QUESTION 186

Identify the access that is initially available to connect to your Database as a Service (DBaaS) environment.

A. Enterprise Manager on port 1158
B. telnet on port 23
C. Cloud Control on port 7799
D. SSH on port 22
E. SSL/TLS on port 443

Correct Answer: D

QUESTION 187

Which statement is true about profiles?

A. Resource limits specified in a profile assigned to a user are always enabled.
B. A user can exist without any profile.
C. A profile can be assigned only to one user.
D. Password management using profiles is always enabled.

Correct Answer: D

QUESTION 188

In your database, the RESOURCE_LIMIT parameter is set to TRUE. You create the profile:

```
CREATE PROFILE app_user LIMIT
SESSIONS_PER_USER 5
CPU_PER_SESSION UNLIMITED
CPU_PER_CALL 3000
IDLE_TIME 10
PASSWORD_LIFE_TIME 60
PASSWORD_REUSE_TIME 60
PASSWORD_REUSE_MAX UNLIMITED
```

Which two statements are true about users and their sessions that are subject to this profile? (Choose two.)

A. The CPU_PER_CALL is ignored in the user sessions because of the unlimited value of CPU_PER_CALL
B. These users can never reuse a password
C. The PASSWORD_LIFE_TIME value is ignored because of the unlimited value of PASSWORD_REUSE_MAX.
D. In each user session, the limit for LOGICAL_READS_PER_SESSION in the same as defined in the DEFAULT profile.

Correct Answer: CD

QUESTION 189

Examine the command:

```
SQL> ALTER SYSTEM SET ENABLE_DDL_LOGGING=TRUE;
```

Which two statements are true in this scenario? (Choose two.)

A. All data definition language (DDL) commands are logged in to the alert log file.
B. All DDL commands are logged in to a text file in Automatic Diagnostic Repository (ADR) home.
C. A subset of executed DDL statements is written into an XML file in ADR home.

D. A subset of executed DDL statements is written to the DDL log in ADR home.

E. All DDL commands are logged in to a trace file in ADR home.

Correct Answer: CD

QUESTION 190

What is the outcome of the SHUTDOWN ABORT command?

A. Pending transactions are committed and the database is closed.
B. Dirtybuffers in the buffer cache and unwritten redo are not written to the data files and redo log files respectively.
C. Uncommitted transactions are rolled back
D. Instance recovery must be requested by the DBA at the next startup

Correct Answer: B

QUESTION 191

Which component resides in the System Global Area (SGA) of a database instance only in shared server connections?

A. User Global Area
B. Program Global Area
C. SQL Query Result Cache
D. PL/SQL Function Result Cache

Correct Answer: A

QUESTION 192

Which three statements are true about Enterprise Manager Database Express? (Choose three.)

A. It can be used to perform database backup operations.
B. It can use the HTTP protocol.
C. The same port number is used for multiple Database Express configurations on the same host.
D. It can use the HTTPS protocol.

E. It is available only when the database is open.

Correct Answer: BDE

QUESTION 193

An application repeatedly accesses small lookup tables, causing a lot of physical I/O operations. What do you recommend to minimize this?
A. Configure the nonstandard buffer cache with a buffer size greater than the size of the default buffer cache.
B. Increase the size of the shared pool
C. Configure the KEEP buffer cache and alter the tables to use the KEEP cache.
D. Configure the RECYCLE buffer cache and alter the tables to use the RECYCLE cache.

Correct Answer: C

QUESTION 194

Your database is open in read/write mode and multiple users are connected to the database instance.

You execute the following command:
```
SQL> ALTER SYSTEM ENABLE RESTRICTED SESSION;
```
What would be the effect on current sessions?

A. They are not terminated but may only issue queries.
B. They are not affected.
C. They are terminated immediately.
D. They are terminated after completing the transaction.

Correct Answer: B

QUESTION 195

You want to distribute a set of structured data to your customers who can integrate this data into their existing databases irrespective of the platform. Which method provides the fastest way of achieving this?

A. using the DBVERIFY utility
B. using direct-path INSERT SQL statements
C. using SQL*Loader
D. using RMAN transportable tablespace operation

Correct Answer: D

QUESTION 196

You create a locally managed tablespace ORDERS_TBS with automatic segment management. You then create the table DAILY_ORDS_LST in the ORDERS_TBS tablespace using the command.

```
CREATE TABLE daily_ords_1st(ordno NUMBER, ord_date
DATE) PCTFREE 20;
```

How does the PCTFREE storage parameter influence data storage for this table?

A. It allows only 80% of space to be occupied in all data blocks of this table.
B. It minimizes row chaining during row insertion.
C. It minimizes row migration during existing row data updation.
D. It automatically coalesces free space of a data block when it reaches 20% of available space.

Correct Answer: A

QUESTION 197

What must you use to read data from a table in your database and write it to an external table?

A. Use SQL* LOADER conventional path load.
B. Use SQL* LOADER direct path load.
C. Use CREATE TABLE. . ORGANIZATION EXTERNAL command with ORACLE_LOADER access driver.
D. Use CREATE TABLE. . ORGANIZATION EXTERNAL command with ORACLE_DATAPUMP access driver.

Correct Answer: D

QUESTION 198

Which two statements are true about initialization parameter files? (Choose two.)

A. A lost or damaged SPFILE can be re-created by using the parameter values listed in the alertlog.
B. A PFILE must exist for an SPFILE to be created.
C. The ALTER SYSTEM command cannot be used to change the value of any parameter if a database instance has started using a PFILE.
D. Both the SPFILE and PFILE must always reside on a file system accessible from the database host server.
E. On startup, by default a database instance always first searches for an SPFILE, and if it does not find any, searches for a PFILE.

Correct Answer: BE

QUESTION 199

You configured the Fast Recovery Area (FRA) for your database. The database instance is in ARCHIVELOG mode. The default location for the archived redo log files is the FRA.

Which two files are removed automatically if space is required in the FRA as per the retention policy? (Choose two.)

A. Archived redo log files that have multiple copies in a different archive location
B. user-managed backups of data files and control files
C. RMAN backups that are obsolete
D. flashback logs

Correct Answer: CD

QUESTION 200

Which statement is true about a database in ARCHIVELOG mode?

A. All backups taken prior to switching to ARCHIVELOG mode can be used to perform complete recovery.
B. Online redo log files have to be multiplexed before putting the database in ARCHIVELOG mode.
C. A Fast Recovery Area (FRA) must be configured for the database.
D. Full database backups can be performed when the database is opened.

Correct Answer: D

QUESTION 201

You want to create a locally managed tablespace called NEWTBS to store segments with different extent sizes. Which set of tablespace attributes can be specified for a tablespace that satisfies the requirements?

A. EXTENT MANAGEMENT LOCAL STORAGE (INITIAL 5M MAXSIZE 10M)
B. REUSE AUTOEXTEND ON MAXSIZE UNLIMITED
C. EXTENT MANAGEMENT LOCAL SEGMENT SPACE MANAGEMENT UNIFORM
D. EXTENT MANAGEMENT LOCAL AUTOALLOCATE

Correct Answer: D

QUESTION 202

The schema SALES exists in two databases, ORCL1 and ORCL2, and has the same password, SALES123. User SALES has CREATE DATABASE LINK and CREATE SESSION privileges on both databases.

Examine these commands:

```
Conn SALES/SALES123
CREATE DATABASE LINK orcl2 USING 'orcl2';
```

What is the outcome of executing these commands in the ORCL1 database?

A. ORCL2 is created as a public database link to connect a single session to the SALES schema in the ORCL2 database.

B. ORCL2 is created as a shared database link to connect multiple sessions to the SALES schema in the ORCL2 database.

C. ORCL2 is created as a private database link to connect to only the SALES schema in the ORCL2 database.

D. ORCL2 database link creation fails.

Correct Answer: C

QUESTION 203

Examine the command:

```
SQL> CONNECT hr/hr@orcl
```

Which two configurations allow this command to execute successfully? (Choose two.)

A. In the tnsnames.ora file, the SERVICE_NAME value of CONNECT_DATA should be explicitly suffixed with the domain name.

B. The SERVICE_NAMES initialization parameter should contain the name orcl in the database host.

C. The orcl TNS alias should be defined such that it is resolvable by a client running on the database host.

D. The orcl TNS alias should be defined in the tnsnames.ora file on both the client and the database host.

E. The TNS_ADMIN environment variable should be set to orcl on the client.

Correct Answer: BC

QUESTION 204

Which three statements are true about Oracle Data Pump? (Choose three.)

A. Oracle Data Pump export and import operations can be performed to move data across different database releases.

B. DBMS_DATAPUMP PL/SQL packages can be used independent of Data Pump clients.

C. A directory object must exist and a user performing an EXPDP or IMPDP operation must have read and write permission on that directory object.

D. Oracle Data Pump export and import operations can be performed only byusers with the SYSDBA privilege.
E. Oracle Data Pump export operations invoked from the clients that are connected remotely by using a connection string, create Data Pump files on the client file system.

Correct Answer: ABC

QUESTION 205

In your database, archive logging and control file autobackup are enabled. The data files and redo log files are intact but control files are impacted due to media failure. In which two recovery scenarios must you use the RESETLOGS option? (Choose two.)

A. One control file copy is intact so the spfile is changed to refer to only one copy.
B. One control file copy is intact and damaged control file copies have to be restored to the default location.
C. All copies of the control file are damaged and the CREATE CONTROLFILE statement is executed manually.
D. All copies of the control file are damaged and the auto backed up control file is used for recovery.
E. One control file copy is intact and damaged control file copies have to be restored to a non-default location.

Correct Answer: CD

QUESTION 206

Which statement is true regarding the DEFAULT profile?

A. The values assigned to the resource limits and password parameters in the default profile can be altered.
B. A different DEFAULT profile can be created before each user in a database.
C. It can be dropped and recreated.
D. it must be explicitly assigned to the user.

Correct Answer: A

QUESTION 207

Your database is running in ARCHIVELOG mode.

You want to take a consistent whole database backup.

Which two statements are true in this scenario? (Choose two.)

A. RMAN backups contain only data files.
B. The database instance must be shut down to take a user-managed consistent backup.
C. Consistent RMAN backups can be taken while the database is open.
D. User-managed backups only contain formatted data blocks.
E. The database must be in MOUNT state to take consistent RMAN backups.

Correct Answer: CD

QUESTION 208

Which background process does Automatic Shared Memory Management use to coordinate the sizing of memory components?

A. PMON
B. SMON
C. MMNL
D. MMAN
E. MMON

Correct Answer: D

QUESTION 209

You enabled block change tracking for faster incremental backups in your database. Which background process writes to the change tracking file?

A. RBAL
B. CKPT
C. SMON
D. PMON

E. MMON
F. CTWR
G. DBWR

Correct Answer: F

QUESTION 210

You configured the flash recovery area in the database. Which two files would you expect to find in the flash recovery area? (Choose two.)

A. backup pieces
B. copies of all parameter files
C. trace file generated using BACKUP CONTROLFILE TO TRACE
D. control file autobackups

Correct Answer: AD

QUESTION 211

Because of a logical corruption in the EMPLOYES tables, you want to perform Tablespace Point-in-Time Recovery (TSPITR) to recover the table. Before you started the TSPITR process, you queried the TS_PITR_CHECK view and you realized that the table has a referential constraint with DEPARTMENTS that exists in another tablespace, MASTERTBS. Which two actions will permit the TSPITR to work? (Choose two.)

A. Taking the MASTERTBS tablespace offline
B. Dropping the relationship between the tables
C. Adding the MASTERTBS tablespace to the recovery set
D. Putting the MASTERTBS tablespace in read-only mode

Correct Answer: BC

Explanation/Reference:

http://docs.oracle.com/cd/E11882_01/backup.112/e10642/rcmtspit.htm#BRADV99978

If constraints for the tables in tablespace tbs1 are contained in the tablespace tbs2, then you cannot recover tbs1 without also recovering tbs2.

QUESTION 212

You executed the following query:

```
SELECT oldest_flashback_scn, oldest_flashback_time
FROM V$FLASHBACK_DATABASE_LOG;
```

Considering that all the redo logs are available, what information can you derive from the output of the preceding query?

A. The time when the last flashback operation in your database was performed
B. The time when the first flashback operation in our database was performed
C. The approximate time and the lowest system change number (SCN) to which you can flash back your database
D. The system change number (SCN) and the time when the Flashback Database was enabled in the database instance

Correct Answer: C

QUESTION 213

To enable faster incremental backups, you enabled block change tracking for the database. Which two statements are true about the block change tracking file? (Choose two.)

A. Multiple change tracking files can be created for a database.
B. The change tracking file must be created after the first level 0 backup.
C. RMAN does not support backup and recovery of the change tracking file.
D. The database clears the change tracking file and starts tracking changes again, after whole database restore and recovery operations.

Correct Answer: CD

QUESTION 214

Which three statements are true about the Pre-Upgrade Information Tool? (Choose three.)

A. It clears all user recycle bins in a database and releases their storage space.
B. It writes a list of invalid SYS and SYSTEM object to the registry$sys_inv_objs table.
C. It evaluates the dependencies of network utility packages.
D. It identifies any deprecated and unsupported parameters.
E. It generates fix-up scripts and automatically runs them to resolve issues that are flagged in the source database.

Correct Answer: BCD

QUESTION 215

You install Oracle Grid Infrastructure standalone server and issue the following command:

```
crsctl start has
```

Which two existing components get automatically added to the Oracle Restart configuration? (Choose two.)

A. Oracle CSSD services
B. the database whose instance is running
C. Oracle Notification services
D. Oracle Healthcheck services
E. Oracle Net Listener

Correct Answer: AC

QUESTION 216

Examine this command executed on a client that is remote from the database server.

```
SQL> CONNECT hr/hr@orcl
```

Which two are required for this command to connect the SQLPLUS client to a database instance? (Choose two.)

A. An `orcl` TNS entry must be defined in the client-side and server-side `tnsnames.ora` files
B. An `orcl` TNS entry must be defined in the client-side `tnsnames.ora` file
C. A service name must be defined to the listener that matches the service name in the `orcl` TNS entry
D. An `orcl` TNS entry must be defined in the server-side `tnsnames.ora` file
E. The service name `orcl` must be defined to the listener

Correct Answer: DE

QUESTION 217

One of your databases supports an OLTP workload. The default `UNDO` tablespace is fixed size with:

1. RETENTION NOGUARANTEE
2. UNDO_RETENTION is 12 minutes

User `SCOTT` gets this error after a query on the SALES table has run for more than 15 minutes:

`ORA-01555: snapshot too old`

Which three factors taken separately or in some combination might be the cause? (Choose three.)

A. An update was made to the SALES table after the query began
B. An update to the SALES table was committed after the query began
C. A committed delete to the SALES table was made more than 12 minutes before the query began
D. An uncommitted update to the SALES table was made more than 12 minutes before the query began
E. A committed update to the SALES table was made more than 12 minutes before the query began

F. An uncommitted delete to the SALES table was made more than 12 minutes before the query began

G. An update was made to the SALES table before the query began

Correct Answer: ADE

QUESTION 218

One of your databases has archive logging enabled and RMAN backups are taken at regular intervals. The data file for the USERS tablespace is corrupt.

Which command must you execute before starting the recovery of this tablespace?

A. STARTUP FORCE
B. ALTER TABLESPACE users OFFLINE IMMEDIATE;
C. SWITCH DATAFILE ALL;
D. ALTER TABLESPACE users OFFLINE NORMAL;
E. ALTER TABLESPACE users OFFLINE TEMPORARY;

Correct Answer: E

QUESTION 219

Which two statements are true about SQL*Loader Express Mode in an Oracle 12c database? (Choose two.)

A. It loads data faster than conventional SQL*Loader
B. No data file needs to be specified
C. It can load data in parallel
D. It loads data more efficiently than conventional SQL*Loader
E. It requires Enterprise Manager Express to be configured

Correct Answer: AC

Explanation/Reference:

https://www.oracle.com/technetwork/database/enterprise-edition/learnmore/sqlldr-express-mode-wp-1991038.pdf

QUESTION 220

Which are two ways for a database service to be recognized by a listener in Oracle Database 12c? (Choose two.)

A. Dynamic Registration by the LREG process
B. Dynamic Registration by the SMON process
C. Static registration in the listener.ora file using the GLOBAL_DBNAME parameter
D. Dynamic Registration by the PMON process
E. Static registration in the listener.ora file using the SERVICE_NAME parameter

Correct Answer: AE Section: (none) Explanation

Explanation/Reference:

https://docs.oracle.com/database/121/NETAG/listenercfg.htm#NETAG298

QUESTION 221

You ran this command on a source database:

```
$> expdp hr/hr DIRECTORY=dumpdir DUMPFILE=emp1.dmp
VIEWS_AS_TABLES=emp_dept
```

On the target database, you run this command:

```
$> impdp hr/hr DIRECTORY=dumpdir DUMPFILE=emp1.dmp
VIEWS_AS_TABLES=emp_dept
```

Which two statements are true? (Choose two.)

A. The expdp operation exports all rows for tables contained in the defining query of the EMP_DEPT view
B. The impdp operation creates separate tables for each table contained in the defining query of the EMP_DEPT view
C. The expdp operation exports all rows that are displayed when querying the EMP_DEPT view with no filter
D. The impdp operation creates EMP_DEPT as a table

E. The `expdp` operation exports the table definitions for tables that are queried in the EMP_DEPT view.
F. The `impdp` operation creates EMP_DEPT as a view

Correct Answer: DE

QUESTION 222

Which four statements are true about database instance behavior? (Choose four.)

A. An idle instance is created when a STARTUP NOMOUNT is successful
B. All dynamic performance views (v$ views) return data when queried from a session connected to an instance in NOMOUNT state
C. The consistency of redo logs and data files is checked when mounting the database
D. Redo log files can be renamed in MOUNT state
E. An SPFILE can be updated when connected to an idle instance
F. Datafiles can be renamed in MOUNT state

Correct Answer: CDEF

QUESTION 223

Examine this command:

```
SQL> ALTER SYSTEM SET ENABLE_DDL_LOGGING=TRUE;
```

Which two statements are true? (Choose two.)

A. All data definition language (DDL) statements are written to the control file
B. Some DDL statements are written to an XML file in the ADR home
C. All DDL statements are logged in to a text file in Automatic Diagnostic Repository (ADR) home
D. Some data definition language (DDL) statements are written to the control file
E. Some DDL statements are written to a text file in the ADR home
F. The Alert Log still contains some DDL statements

Correct Answer: DE